A
TRUE
STORY
OF A
DRUNKEN
MOTHER

Nancy Lee Hall

South End Press
Boston, MA

To all my children who lovingly and patiently raised me,
and to all my sisters who still suffer.

Acknowledgement is gratefully extended to the following women:
Margaret Roberts, Josephine Lauer, Martha McAuliffe, Meredith
Campbell, Rosan Sullivan Staubach, Frances Bardacke, Diane Sinor,
and in memory, Gloria Ellsworth.

Library of Congress Cataloging-in Publication Data
Hall, Nancy Lee.
    A true story of a drunken mother / Nancy Lee Hall.
    p. cm.
    ISBN 0-89608-381-0 $25.00 -- ISBN 0-89608-380-2 (pbk.)
$8.00
    I. Title.
    PS3558.A372T78   1990
    813'.54--dc20
    Library of Congress card number: 90-9542 CIP

text design by Loretta Li
cover illustration by Bob Diven
printed on acid-free paper

South End Press, 116 St. Botolph St., Boston, MA 02115
99 98 97 96 95 94 93 92 91 90 1 2 3 4 5 6 7 8 9 10

Introduction to the first edition:

As of September 6, 1973 I have been sober fifteen years. I struggled with six of my seven children for ten years–alone. But I have not been alone in the last five. I have had support, love, and untiring help from my sisters in the movement. They have helped me through the prejudice I faced as a divorcee, work and legal problems, evictions from rented houses, welfare, and a lot more. My oldest son spent four years in the Air Force and my second son went to Vietnam.

All of my sisters were present at my fifteenth-year birthday party along with my children. I have a good job as a draftswoman and I have nothing but love in my heart for the movement and my many friends.

Nancy Lee Hall
1974

Introduction to the second edition:

It has been sixteen years since this book was first published by Daughters, Inc., one of the first feminist publishing companies in the seventies. Now, in 1990, after my thirty-two years of sobriety, it is in print again. I have had more than a little help from my friends and the courageous people at South End Press who continue, against all odds, to publish the truth.

Many changes have taken place in our American culture and now our obsession is with the WAR ON DRUGS. How did we get here? Well, here's a little history—

In 1955, at Alcoholics Anonymous' twentieth anniversary, Bill Wilson (as we all know, there is no more anonymity), a co-founder of AA, spoke to a large audience:

> When we first come into AA we find here, as we have observed before, a greater personal freedom than any other society knows. We cannot be compelled to do anything. In that sense, this society is a benign anarchy. I think the Russian Prince who so strongly advocated that idea felt that if men (and today—women) were granted absolute liberty, and were compelled to obey no one in person, they would associate themselves in common interest.

When AA began in 1935, and for years afterward, hospitals wanted nothing to do with alcoholics or drug addicts. Gradually, the medical profession acknowledged the success of the AA movement, whose primary purpose was to help one another stay sober (for free). AA didn't boast a "cure" for alcoholism; it simply provided a supportive group and a model program drunks could use to better their lives.

The once condemning doctors and their hospitals, observing the success of AA, began to willingly open their doors to drunks and drug addicts (for a price) under the guise of being able to make them clean and sober people. The truth is that no one can get anyone clean and sober—and make them stay that way. Today, we know this attempt as "treatment." Treatment tries to do for addicts something they can only do for themselves. It relies on people's fear of authority rather than helping them to find their own source of power.

Treatment has become one of the most profitable capitalistic ventures of modern times. It's so profitable it might replace WAR. And buzz words such as co-dependent, enabler, co-enabler, denial, intervention, and adult child of an alcoholic have become a part of our everyday language.

With few real rehabilitation successes, the hospitals finally realized that the AA program was vital to their treatment plans. So they began holding AA meetings in hospitals. Adding to this, they purchased vans and buses to drive large numbers of patients directly to AA meetings in the community. AA, being an Anarchy, has tried to absorb and help these people (for free) but some members have expressed to me that the quality of the meetings is suffering. They wonder, at times, just how many of these people are real addicts or alcoholics.

These treatment programs are costly—from $10,000 for a twenty-eight day program to $35,000 and up for the more posh country clubs. Most people who go to treatment programs have insurance. This excludes poor people who may want help but have no money.

In order for substance abuse programs to continue they must have a product and that product is YOU and ME. How in the world did they convince us that we are ALL sick and need help? Contemporary sophisticated propaganda has communicated to a large majority of the people exactly what Bertram Gross writes in his book, *Friendly Fascism*. 1. You are deficient. 2. You have a problem. 3. You have a collection of problems.

The professionals, in turn, are the "loving" or "caring" problem-solvers. They teach confused people that they will be better helped because the professionals "know" better. Only rarely does a therapist allow attention to be focused on the many sources of anxiety and misery that lie in the political, economic, and social sphere.

I interviewed several people who had been in treatment and women, once again, told me some real horror stories about being abused by male therapists. It seems we have not yet learned from Phyllis Chesler's *Women and Madness*. And a man in treatment remarked:

> I asked why I couldn't talk about Nicaragua and the therapist said, "Oh, there's nothing we can do about that. Just don't think about it. You just concentrate on yourself."

There is no scientifically proven medical treatment for addiction, so what are these hospitals treating? Just from my own experience I know that if you are an addict (I include alcohol), only abstinence can arrest your addiction. Then who is an addict? Only YOU know and although you may need a few days in a hospital to detox, AA and NA (Narcotics Anonymous) are FREE.

From a historical perspective, nineteenth-century America was a "dope fiend's paradise." Opium was on sale and at low prices throughout the century. Physicians dispensed opiates directly, drugstores sold them over the counter, grocery and general stores routinely stocked and sold opiates. And for users unable to patronize the stores, they were sent by mail. Finally, there were countless patent medicines on the market containing opium and morphine. They were sold under such names as Ayers Cherry Pectoral, Mrs. Winslow's Soothing Syrup, Darby's Carminative, Godfrey's Cordial, McMunn's Elixir of Opium and Dover's Powder—to name just a few. They were widely advertised in the newspapers for use as teething syrups, pain-killers, cough mixtures, cures for diarrhea, dysentery, and "women's problems."

At that time drugs were not viewed as a menace to society; they were not, in fact, a menace. The cultivation of the opium poppy was not banned until 1942.

One Massachusetts druggist, asked to review his opiate sales, added a picturesque detail. He had only one steady customer, he reported, and that was "a noted temperance lecturer."

In reviewing the history of drugs, I found two things helping to promote drug use and addiction. The first is misclassifying drugs and the second is making more and more stringent laws. Every time the laws get stricter, drug use soars. Prohibition doesn't work because there's too much money to be made.

But what I see as the greatest problem of all is the scare tactics being used on our people and the fear that has been instilled in others about DRUG ADDICTS. Why have we put so much emphasis on drugs without including alcohol, nicotine, caffeine, legal drugs, or the chemicals all around us in our daily lives?

Our government is doing its best to divert us from the real social problems: poverty, homelessness, the environment, education, sexism, racism, ageism, and many more.

The rich pay no taxes and the rest of us pick up the bill. With our money, wars are started in tiny countries that are trying to free themselves from us and then the president espouses a kinder, gentler nation. We put drug addicts in jail and prisons and give permission to the medical profession to dispense the same drugs, legally. We have more people in prisons than any other country in the world except South Africa—and Nixon, Reagan, North, and that gang never even see the bars. If I try to talk politics to anyone, they say, "Oh, that's so depressing. I don't want to think about politics." It's all about money.

Not many professionals in the treatment business want to hear about my long-term sobriety because they depend on recidivism. They approve when judges sentence people to go to treatment centers. They don't mind if kids turn in their parents or parents turn in their kids or corporations turn in their workers to get rid of agitators or if people get hooked on the drugs they're given in treatment hospitals or if teens are taken to psychiatric hospitals because their parents think they're hard-core addicts and don't know what to do. We are taught to despise the young black kid selling drugs who wants to be a capitalist the way we have showed him. It's all just fine because we can make television movies about all the problems!

I interviewed a druggist and her mind was already made up. She said, *"I* don't sell needles to *addicts!"*

I said, "How do you know whether or not they're addicts?

She hesitated. "Well, I guess I really don't know but I don't want to take a chance. Also, I know there are drugstores that will sell to them."

I tried to point out that she was being put in a position to be judge and jury without the person having a trial and maybe if the person was an addict, clean needles might prevent AIDS. She agreed to take another look at her position.

I left a job at Sundstrand Corporation because their drug policy stated they could search my car, my desk, my purse, and my clothing at any time.

I am not trying to downplay the seriousness of addiction—it is ravaging to the addict. But I resent the political use of my brothers and sisters, who are addicts, to make billions for the treatment industry.

With all the legal drugs we have now, I am for the legalization of all drugs so we can stop being so hypocritical. Let addicts out of prison and provide them with a decent living wage and opportunities to live as human beings. People concerned about drug abuse and alcoholism should organize to challenge the political and economic pressures on addicts.

I am so grateful for the people who helped me and gave me total freedom to make mistakes along the way. If I was forced into treatment today I would probably die rather than surrender my creativity, my mind, and my soul to people who, themselves, are imperfect. I will not be made out of a cookie cutter and come out like everyone else. Who guards the guards?

The philosophy of AA is as old as humankind. It is about caring and loving each other no matter who we are or what we do. Every addict deserves a chance to be sober so if my book hits you, get a little help from your friends. To the rest I say: LOVE AN ADDICT TODAY!

Nancy Lee Hall
March 1990

1

Many times, over the years, I tried to kill myself. I remember one time in particular:

Federal and Navy housing had all been the same. Every place I'd lived, for ten years, had been the same—a dump. I had no hope left because I could see no possibility of change.

Karl, my Navy Chief husband, was gone again. I was drunk again. And my six children were frightened—again.

I stumbled to the kitchen sink, brushed the cockroaches away, and poured another glass of wine. When it hit my stomach, I shuddered.

The television was on and the lights were out. I sat down in a chair and knocked a baby bottle off the arm. Broken glass and sour milk scattered on the bare floor. I didn't care. I staggered to the refrigerator, opened it, and saw only one bottle of formula left. I didn't care. I went back to the chair to watch television and the screen looked divided in two. Holding my hand over one eye, I forced the picture into focus.

My mind raced again and I drank another glass of wine. I bumped my way to the first bedroom and saw Mary and Susan sleeping and I cried. In the second bedroom I saw Chris, Tim, and David—sleeping. Then I stumbled into my own bedroom to check my baby, Steve.

The blankets were over his head and I quickly jerked them back. I stood there motionless. Was he dead? I jiggled him a little and he let out a faint cry.

What have I done to my children?

I went back to the dark living room and held up the half-gallon wine bottle. It was almost empty. One more drink and that would be it. It dribbled down my chin and onto my already wine-stained housedress. The decision was made. My mind was made up: I would do it. I put a towel across the crack at the bottom of the front door, turned on all the gas burners, shut off the television, and lay down on the brown leather couch.

There. It's done. It's no use. Everybody will be better off. It's all right. It's all going to be over. It's all right. Gas. Smell gas. Can't go on. I want to die. Kill myself. Yes. Yes. Kill all the kids? Oh, God! No! Oh, no! I don't have the right. I have no right. Better get up. Get up. I can't. I can't move. Get up! Get up! Turn it off! Get up!

I fell off the couch, got to my knees, and crawled to the stove. I reached up, shut off the burners, and pulled myself up to open the front door.

I hit most of the furniture getting to the bedroom, pulled a fresh fifth of wine from under the mattress, opened it, sat on the floor, and gulped. In my final attempt to move around, I fell and conked my eye on the gas heater that sat by the wall in the small dirty living room.

When I woke up, it was morning and I was surprised to find myself in my own bed. Usually I passed out on the couch.

How did I get here? What's happening? Oh God I feel sick! Why didn't I die? The baby, the kids, a bottle for the baby. I can't move. I've got to have a drink—I can't stand the hurting! If I have one drink I'll feel better. But how did I get here, in my own bed?

In bits and pieces my mind vaguely put together the night before.

I was on the floor looking up at Chris's blond hair falling over his eyes and Mary's torn pajamas. Oh. . .now I remember. . .they were tugging and pulling me.

Chris whispered, "I guess she's a goner this time."

When I realized they had lifted me onto my bed, I pulled the pillow around my face and sobbed.

After several minutes, the sobbing stopped and the pain started. I wrapped my arms around my belly and walked, stooped over, to the bathroom. I tried to vomit and nothing came up. I got on my knees and held tight to the toilet seat. Finally, like a volcano erupting, it all came up and the toilet was full of blood. The vomiting took my breath away and my heart pounded. When nothing more would come, I slowly raised my head and very carefully stood up. For the first time in many years, I looked at myself in the mirror—really looked.

Oh my God!

My eyes looked like marbles. My face was swollen and covered with red blotchy sores. One eye was black and purple from hitting the gas heater. My hair was long and matted. My lips were white, except for bleeding cracks. I was naked.

Mary was carefully heating the last baby bottle and Chris was saying, "Don't worry. Come on, eat your cereal," to his three brothers and sisters at the kitchen table.

What had happened to me? How in the hell did I
get here?

* * *

The apartment seemed so big to me but I was six and
everything looked big. From the kitchen I could see my
dad sleeping. On those mornings he had an awful smell.
My mother had been gone all night and my brother
Jimmy, who was four, was hungry.

"I want something to eat," Jimmy whined.

I took the milk bottle out of the refrigerator, but when
I tried to open it the cardboard cap squished down into
the bottle.

"I can't do it!" I screamed.

Dad came running.

"What's the matter?"

"I can't do it. I can't open the milk right and Jimmy's
hungry."

"I want my milk!"

"Tell him to shut up, Daddy."

Dad poured two glasses of milk.

"Come on, kids, don't fight. Daddy's head hurts."

He slowly worked his way back to the bed and fell.

* * *

When Mom and Dad got their divorce I was glad. I was
sick of their fighting and screaming at each other. At
Grandma's house, Jimmy and I could have fun. Maybe
Grandma would help me take care of Jimmy. He was
such a worry.

Upstate New York was beautiful and Rochester, where
Grandpa lived, was a fast-growing city. It grew around
the parks, the woods, and hills. Lilac Park would be
there forever. Every year people came from all over to
see the lilacs bloom.

Grandpa—Grandma insisted that we call him Doctor
John—was a dentist and drove a 1930 tan Packard with
bear rugs on the floor. Grandma cooked good meals and
bought Jimmy and me new clothes. Mother found a secretarial job and spent most of her spare time going out
on dates.

One evening I stretched across the blue satin comfort-
er and watched my mother put on a red velvet evening
gown, diamond earrings, and red shoes.

"How do I look, dear?"

"You look pretty."

My mother was beautiful. She was four foot eleven, thin, and her thick auburn hair was wrapped in braids around the top of her head. She always wore the newest fashions but her love for jewelry annoyed me. I never liked jewelry.

She leaned over and kissed me on the forehead.

"Now jump into bed like a good girl."

As I was pulling the covers over me, I heard Doctor John yelling. I sneaked to the banister to watch and listen. Doctor John looked like Abraham Lincoln pacing up and down in front of the fireplace and Grandma, short and fat, sat submissively, knitting, in her rocker.

Doctor John waved his big cigar. "Nora, I don't want you going out with this man."

"It's my life!" Mother exclaimed.

"You just got rid of one drunk and I won't have you getting mixed up with another one."

"He's not a drunk."

"I happen to know different."

Grandma got up, saying, "Are you going to put these children through another mess?"

"I'm not putting them through anything."

Doctor John was angry. "My money paid for your divorce," he said, "and you're living in my house. I will not stand by and watch these children brought up improperly. I don't know where we failed with you. We gave you everything."

A horn tooted.

"There he is. If you won't let him come in, I'll meet him outside."

Grandpa fumed and Mother ran out.

During the night, I had a bad dream and woke up screaming. Grandma came in and consoled me and then I heard her calling Mother on the phone.

"She's your daughter!"

Mother leaned over me, holding a glass of water and two aspirin tablets.

"Here, take these."

I took the aspirin and then watched the red velvet disappear through the door. I lay in the dark, listening to Mother and Grandmother arguing.

"She's your child and you have no business leaving her every night. You're shameful!"

"Mother, will you stop this nonsense? I'm going back to the party."

Mother ran out and my Grandma hollered after her, "Someday you'll be sorry!"

I didn't know what it all meant. I was afraid when they argued about me. I cried myself to sleep.

*   *   *

The street where Doctor John lived was lined with maple trees. On summer evenings men sat on their porches, watching the children playing in the street and on the lawns, and listening to roundtopped radios. Neighbors spoke to each other. Women sat with the men, rocking or sewing. Grandma had a habit of falling asleep.

The first summer at Doctor John's was fun. Jimmy and I climbed the cherry tree in the backyard. It took me practically all summer to get up the courage to jump from the tree to the garage roof. Jimmy sat on a limb, cheering me on.

As we grew, Jimmy didn't seem to have the energy I had. I made new friends and Jimmy had no one. We all played ball in the street and Jimmy just sat on the curb and watched. I felt sorry for him because he was so little and frail but when he decided to follow my girlfriends and me around all the time it made me angry. Was I to be responsible for him forever?

Doctor John was still furious with Mother and the arguing continued. During one big ballgame I saw Mother run down the sidewalk and get into a car with a man. I always tried to put unpleasant things out of my mind but this time I was simply hoping that the other kids wouldn't notice. This time, the sound of Doctor John's police whistle came none too soon.

The police whistle had come into being when Doctor John couldn't yell loud enough to find me.

"From now on when you hear this whistle you'd better get home immediately. I'm only going to blow it once."

I ran into the house as fast as I could. Grandma was bustling around getting the food on the table.

"Wash your hands and get ready to eat, Nancy."

Doctor John always sat at the head of the table, Jimmy and Mother on one side, me on the other, and at the foot Grandma, who sat down last. Mother's place was empty.

"I don't understand your mother," Grandma said. "She's never home any more. She's always running out with that Howard."

"Could we please have our meals with less talking?" Doctor John asked.

For a minute there was silence. Then Grandma started again. "Nancy, why don't you play with Jimmy. He's always going to his room by himself. Poor boy. I feel sorry for him."

"I ask him to play baseball but he doesn't want to do that. He only wants to follow me around when I'm with my girlfriends."

"I don't want to follow you and your girlfriends. What do I care about girls?" he whined.

"Oh, Jimmy, don't tell me. I see you chasing along behind when we go to the drugstore."

"Here, here, Nancy. You can be a little nicer to him," Grandma said.

"I like Jimmy. It's not that I don't like him. I just wish he'd play ball with us. We could use more people."

"I don't like baseball."

"Well, I do."

"Please pass the butter, and be quiet! I don't want to hear another word during this meal. Is that clear?" said Doctor John.

I had so many things left to say.

I finished eating and ran out the front door. Jimmy ran after me. A car was parked across the street and my girlfriend yelled out the window, "Come on, Nancy, my dad's going to take us to the drugstore."

I jumped into the car and we drove away. I looked out the back window just in time to see a big black car hitting Jimmy. I put my head in my hands and didn't say a word.

The corner drugstore with the wirebacked chairs was the favorite hangout of all the kids in the neighborhood. I ordered the largest dish of ice cream the store had and finished it very quickly.

"Do you want another dish?" my girlfriend's father asked.

"If it's okay," I said, sheepishly.

The second dish I ate even faster.

"Nancy, I never saw you eat so much ice cream," my girlfriend said.

I finished off the second dish. "I'm full now," I said. "It sure was good."

They drove me back to my house and I didn't want to go in.

Inside the house, Grandma was weeping.

"They've taken Jimmy to the hospital. He got hit by a car. It's bad and he's hurt badly. I'm trying to reach your mother."

"Where's Doctor John?" I asked.

"He went to the hospital." Grandma blew her nose on her lace handkerchief. "Oh dear! He got hit right out in front of our house!"

Grandma went to the telephone and I was getting sick to my stomach.

It was my fault. I never really wanted him to play with us.

It was many weeks before Jimmy came home from the hospital and no one knew if he would fully recover from the fractured skull and broken bones. I didn't eat much.

Jimmy had to stay in bed for a long time and I never got another chance to ask him to play baseball.

2 Because of his confinement, Jimmy became interested in drawing and art. Watching Jimmy draw was not my idea of excitement. I had so much excess energy that sitting still was not one of my favorite things to do. In fact, during the summer months, I ran, played, and jumped so hard that I experienced terrible nightmares. The doctor finally said I had to take a nap every afternoon, all summer long.

As soon as Grandma closed her bedroom door, I jumped up and down on her big brass bed as though it were a trampoline.

Jimmy was eight, I was ten, and it was the winter of 1933. Doctor John was complaining about the snow I brought in and Grandma, being aware of my energy, suggested that he take me ice skating. Grandma got down Mother's old ice skates and Doctor John drove me to the rink. He stuffed the toes with newspaper, laced up the skates, and guided me to the edge of the ice.

"Let me alone. I can go by myself."

He let go of my arm and I skated away with supreme confidence. Doctor John stood on the bank hitting his arms to keep warm. About a half hour later he waved me in. I didn't want to stop, but I couldn't wait to get home and tell Grandma.

"Grandma, you should see me ice skate. I love it and I want to go every day. Can I please?"

"That's nice, dear. I remember when I used to skate."

Grandma picked up the bottom of her printed housedress and began twirling around the room. "It was the winter of 1896. I had graduated from Neff College of Oratory and Mind Development the previous year. I was the belle of the ice and all the boys were after me. It was that winter I met Forest, a boy I almost married instead of Doctor John. But his family thought he should finish college first. Too bad! He was a looker! Come to think of it, I was valedictorian of my graduating class."

I'd never really known Grandma before and I was very impressed by what she said.

She is really smart, I thought.

Doctor John stopped her from talking by ordering his supper and when I asked him if I could go skating every day he said it would depend on how much housework I accomplished.

Mother came home for supper and gave Jimmy and me

a kiss. Once again the argument started. Mother said she was leaving with Howard and Doctor John told her she wasn't going anywhere with "that man." Mother pushed her chair back and called Jimmy and me into the living room.

"I love you both very much and I'd like to have you come and live with us but it has to be your decision."

It was all so confusing and frightening to me. I picked up one of my skates and started to polish the blade with the bottom of my skirt. Jimmy said he would go with Mother and Howard but when she asked me I didn't know what to say. I stared at Mother. I thought about ice skating. I wondered where Mother was going to live, and, most of all, whether she had any money. Even at that age, I knew Doctor John had money.

"If it's all right with you, Mother, I think I'll stay with Doctor John."

"It's all right with me, Nancy. You can come and visit us any time you'd like to."

Doctor John was standing in the doorway. He said, "And you, Nora, are going to obey me for once. You are not going with 'that man.' "

"I'm sorry, Father, but Howard and I are already married and I'm going with him—now. For God's sake, Dad, I'm thirty-four years old."

"If you leave my house, don't you ever speak to me again!"

Mother's eyes were full and Grandma was crying.

Howard came for Mother and Jimmy. Grandma continued crying. Doctor John was angrier than I had ever seen him. It scared me. After the front door closed, Grandma cried louder and Doctor John lost all of his composure.

"Shut up!" he shouted. "For God's sake shut up! I'm going to bed!"

* * *

It didn't bother me much that Jimmy and Mother were gone. I didn't have to listen to any more arguments and I didn't have to feel scared as long as I obeyed Doctor John. It was getting more and more difficult—he seemed so unreasonable.

He knew that ice skating had become a way of life for me. Even before the first snowfall I lay in bed, looking out the window at the clear round moon, and praying for freezing weather. I never wanted anything so much in my life. Every day after school I sneaked to the rink to see if the ice was forming and every morning before school, I checked Doctor John's antique thermometer on the front porch.

I told him I didn't want piano lessons but he made me take them anyway and threatened to stop my skating if I didn't practice my hour every afternoon after school.

"Skating is a sport. You have to do something constructive with your time. This skating thing is an obsession with you."

"I'm practicing for the speed skating competition and I'm going to win. Some day I'm going to the Olympics."

"You're not going to do anything unless I give you permission. We had the same trouble with your mother but you'd better get it into your head, young lady, that I'm the boss around here and you'll do what I say."

I looked at this six-foot-two man and his stiff white detachable collar and I hated him.

Is this what Mother hated too?

I spent my summers playing sandlot baseball, riding horseback, playing tennis, and generally being as active as possible. Every winter I practiced skating and moved so fast that, even in below-zero weather, sweat dripped off my body.

I stayed out of Doctor John's way as much as possible but it wasn't long before we had a serious altercation.

Mark was a school friend who kept asking me to skate with him. I was fourteen and hadn't yet thought too much about boys and especially didn't want to break training to skate with one. Mark was persistent and I finally gave in. He took my arm and we were skating.

I had looked at myself naked in the mirror, and seen my breasts developing. I had examined my own body regularly, wondering what it was all about but I was more interested in my leg muscles—they could carry me over the line, a winner! I had some vague idea, from bathing with Jimmy, what boys looked like. When I started menstruating I was ashamed. I had no idea what was happening and I hid my bloody pants in my closet. Grandma must have found them because she bought me a box of Kotex and a belt. She handed them to me and said, "You'll be doing this once a month. All women do. It's just our curse." That was everything I knew about sex.

Mark locked his arm in mine and squeezed my hand. It felt good and I was in love.

I asked Doctor John if I could go to the movies with Mark.

"You're entirely too young to go out on a date. I don't even know this boy."

"He's a nice boy and he just wants to take me to the movies."

"How do I know that? Boys have ideas. I'll have to think about it. When is this big affair supposed to take place?"

"Tomorrow night."

He handed me a book from the bookcase. "In the meantime I want you to read and study this book thoroughly."

It was a blue book, called *Growing Up*.

What did he think I was going to do? He didn't trust me at all. Of course I had been scared, a long time ago, when the nasty boy down the street cornered me in the garage and asked me what my hole looked like, but Mark wasn't like him at all. I looked at the book again. Baby stuff!

I looked at myself in the mirror. I was ready for my first date. Red sweater, red skirt, white socks and saddle shoes. The night before I had pinned my hair up in a hundred pin curls and was trying to comb and fix it to look right.

I wondered if I smelled good. I picked up a bottle of cologne and poured some on my arm, and behind my ear.

Whew, that was strong.

I ran downstairs to show Grandma and she said I looked very pretty. Doctor John was sitting in his Morris chair, as usual, smoking his cigar. Every time I wanted something I had to go to that Morris chair, the throne. He said he wouldn't let me go unless Mark came into the house and I introduced him.

"And I want you home at ten."

"But what if the movie isn't over then?"

"You heard me, and besides I want you to start packing some of your things tomorrow—we're moving to the country."

I couldn't believe what I'd heard. Moving? What about my skating, my school, Mother and Jimmy? I yelled at Doctor John and he just told me that he'd had a hard day at the office and didn't want to discuss it. I ran upstairs to my room, slammed the door, plopped on the bed, and cried. My whole life was destroyed. I had my first boyfriend and skating was going very well. Now Doctor John was moving us all to the country. How could he do this to me? Grandma came in and sat on the edge of my bed.

"It'll be all right. You can see Jimmy once in a while."

"How can I practice my skating? Why is he doing this? He's so mean."

"We have to do what he says. After all, he is a good provider."

"Can I go and live with Mother?"

"I'm afraid not, dear. Nora is having a great deal of financial trouble. Howard isn't working and it's all Nora can do to work and support them—let alone have an extra mouth to feed. You wouldn't want to live like that after the good life we've given you. Now would you?"

"I wouldn't care if I didn't have anything as long as I could skate in the competition. I hate him. I hate Grandpa."

"You mustn't say that. He's done a lot for all of us."

"Grandma, do you want to move to the country?"

"The Bible tells us we must go where our husbands go."

"But do you really want to go?"

"That doesn't matter. It's what I must do."

"But you won't see your close friends or Mrs. Clark any more."

Grandma turned her face away. "I'll miss them," she said. "Come, Nancy. Mark will be here to pick you up. Comb your hair and come downstairs."

Mark took my hand and we walked to the movies. He held my hand all through the picture and I just knew that I loved him.

When we came out, it was already ten. Mark hurried me down the street, past all the store windows to get me home on time.

"Gee, everything's so bright and exciting, isn't it?"

"Your grandfather's going to be mad at me."

"I don't care. I want to see things."

Mark walked into the vestibule with me. The house was dark. We stood facing each other for a moment and then he quickly kissed me on the lips and ran out. I put my head back against the wall and the whole house lit up.

"Well, young lady, I guess you know that you're half an hour late?"

"But, Doctor John, the movie was just over," I pleaded.

"I warned you, so now you're restricted from skating until further notice."

I begged, "Please, please don't do that. I have to train for the competition. Please, Doctor John. You don't really mean it, do you?"

"You bet I do. I know boys and girls when they get alone at night. That boy's up to no good. What did he try to do?"

What did he mean? Kissing couldn't hurt.

"Nothing, honest."

"Go to bed this instant."

I could feel my hurt turning to rage and I ran up to my bedroom and locked the door. I pulled all the covers off the bed and threw them out the window. Then the pillows, my clothes, the rugs, my dressing table stool, and finally my mattress. Doctor John knocked on the door and I wouldn't answer. He demanded, screamed, and threatened me and I still wouldn't go out.

"All right. Stay in there as long as you like, but you'll get hungry."

I put my ear to the door and heard him walk downstairs. I threw myself on the floor and cried. I knew he'd make me, somehow, carry everything back up in the morning.

3 Moving to the country was the most dreadful experience I had for I knew my life had ended and I hated Doctor John and even Grandma for letting him move. Now I was a real rebel. I would get even some day—in some way.

My rebellion took a strange form and it suited me fine. In my new red brick schoolhouse, that smelled of cow manure because most of the boys had to milk before coming to school, I was instantly popular. I was different from all the other hundred-and-twenty-five kids. They had lived in the country most of their lives, but I was a "city girl." At lunchtime I talked everyone into going down behind the railroad station to smoke, drink beer, and swim nude in the wide river. I made friends with all the boys who had Model Ts and Model As because that was the only way to get around in the country. I introduced Doctor John to a couple of girls and on weekends I told him I was going to a girl's house. The girl would pick me up and then we would meet the boys down the road and go to the local roadhouse.

One night I spotted an older boy at the bar. He glanced at me and then asked me to dance. I had drunk about four bottles of beer and was feeling silly. I leaned all over him while the country music blared.

Suddenly the whole room started to go around. I said, "Excuse me," but before I could get to the front door I fell down and passed out. When I came to, I had no idea how I'd gotten into a car or even whose car it was.

I looked up and saw the boy.

"Feel better now?"

"Wow! I guess so. What happened?"

"You passed out on the floor."

"How'd I get here?"

"It's my car. I carried you out."

"Could you please take me home?"

"Sure."

Harry was twenty-one and tall and blond. I found out that his father owned a farm and Harry worked for him. He didn't dress like the other kids—he wore a sport shirt and slacks. He was more the city type. He asked if he could call me sometime and I said yes. At that moment, though, I just wanted to get home. It was two-thirty in the morning and Doctor John was waiting again.

16 "You have been drinking! After all the trouble we've

had with drunks! Well, you won't go out with that crew any more."

By now I really didn't care what he was saying. I would just have to take my punishment in the morning, But then I was too sick to care. Life had cheated me already and I was just fifteen.

I wondered if I'd ever get to skate again.

The next day was Saturday and when I came downstairs Grandma was standing, looking out the window. She recited,

> The dead they sleep, a long, long sleep;
> The dead they rest, and their rest is deep;
> The dead have peace, but the living weep.

I had never seen her act so odd. "What's the matter, Grandma?"

"You see that light? That red light far away? That's where the communists live. Come here, I'll show you."

"I don't see any light. How can you see a light so far away in the daytime?"

"I can see it. That's the way they work it. It's just for me to see."

"Where's Doctor John?"

"With his chickens," she answered laughingly.

Her eyes had a wild look and I was glad to see Doctor John come in the house. He told her it was time to go and to get her suitcase. In minutes he was driving off in his Packard with Grandma in the back seat. Nothing was said to me and I remained puzzled. While he was gone I made the beds and did the dishes, knowing that with his new problem, he would forget all about punishing me.

For the next few weeks I helped Doctor John. Harry called several times but I was afraid to ask Doctor John if I could go out with him. Maybe if just worked real hard he would give me permission. It was summer vacation, and staying home all the time was a real bore.

Then one Sunday Doctor John told me that he wanted to take me to visit Grandma. All I knew was that she was in a hospital. Still trying to get on the good side of him, I agreed.

He drove up in front of a building and I immediately saw the sign that read, "New York State Hospital."

I got out of the Packard and Doctor John drove away,
shouting that he would pick me up after visiting hours. I

went to the desk and asked to see Grandma. A nurse with a large ring of keys hanging from her waist led me to a door. She unlocked the door, and then another door, and pointed to where Grandma was sitting. She was in a chair, her back to me, and her hair hung down below her waist.

I'd never seen Grandma with her hair down. She'd always worn it in a bun at the back of her neck. This must be a mental institution, I thought.

"Grandma?"

When she turned around, I froze. She had a silly grin on her face and didn't even know who I was.

"My sister hung herself in the attic. Are you my sister?" Grandma rambled.

"No, Grandma, I'm Nancy."

Grandma recited:

And yet they say we live secure at home, while they are at the wars, with their sorry reasoning, for I would gladly take my stand in battle array three times o'er than once give birth. But enough! this language suits not thee as it does me; thou hast a city here, a father's house, some joy in life, and friends to share thy thoughts, but I am destitute, without a city, and therefore scorned by my husband, a captive from a foreign shore, with no mother, brother, or kind man in whom to find a new haven of refuge from this calamity.

I couldn't do anything except listen to her babbling. The nurse announced that it was time for the patients to smoke. They followed the nurse to a room and I asked her if I could go too. I really needed a cigarette! We all piled into a little room and the nurse took the matches out of her pocket to light everyone's cigarette. I took a big drag and listened.

"What kinda crap are you telling me?" one girl said.

"I said I'd screwed more guys than you had," the other answered.

"You goddamn bitch! You have not! You don't even know what you're talking about!"

The nurse said, "All right, girls! Stop fighting!"

I finished my cigarette and went back to Grandma. By now Grandma was mumbling incoherently so I just

18

watched the patients rocking, chanting, praying, and dancing.

Visiting hours were over, the nurse announced.

"Goodbye, Grandma."

Grandma motioned for me to kneel down in front of her. She whispered in my ear: "Be free, pretty young girl. Be free."

The nurse unlocked all the doors again for the visitors to leave. Doctor John was waiting and we didn't speak all the way home.

4 In the fall Grandma came home from the hospital, seemingly normal. I had spent a great deal of time getting on the good side of Doctor John and when I asked him if I could go out with Harry, he gave in. I was very careful not to tell him how old Harry was.

Harry drove a 1936 Ford and sitting beside Harry made me feel fully grown. I couldn't wait to grow up.

Someday I'd be able to get away from Doctor John. He just didn't understand me. And Grandma always stuck up for him because she was scared of him too. Maybe Mother was right to run away from Doctor John. She wasn't much better off with Howard though. I knew one thing—I was going to do something. I was not going to be like Grandma and Mother.

I wanted to share my enthusiasm about skating with Harry but he was totally uninterested. Whenever we'd go out to the movies or to roadhouses to drink we'd always end up parking down a country lane. He told me over and over again that he loved me and I liked everything except the fact that he never wanted to hear about my skating.

"If you really loved me, you'd be interested."

He pulled me to him again. "I'll show you how much I love you."

He put his hand on my leg and tried to put my hand on his hard penis. "Come on, I won't hurt you. How much longer do you think I can stand this?"

"I can't, Harry. Please! Stop!"

It wasn't that I didn't want to. I was petrified that if I did Doctor John would somehow find out and literally kill me. He had made it very clear that it was wrong to do anything with boys. He and Grandma had separate bedrooms and I knew that they never made love. I had a hard time picturing them making love even when they were younger.

Harry stopped abruptly and started the car. "Okay. Okay."

Harry gave me a quick kiss as I got out of his car to go into the house. I went to bed that night with mixed thoughts.

If I didn't let him do it pretty soon, he'd stop taking me out. How could I get out of this house for good? Maybe I could go live with Mother. How was I going to get to the city to practice before the competition in

January? Then it hit me. I could take a bus into town on the weekends and stay with Mother. She'd like that. Besides, I hadn't seen her or Jimmy in a long time. Yes. That's what I'd do. I'd ask Grandma to talk to Doctor John.

Pleased with myself, I turned over and fell asleep.

* * *

Nothing was discussed until the freeze.

Doctor John's argument was that the creek was frozen near our house and he couldn't understand why I didn't want to practice on it. I told him there was a practice track at the rink in the city and once again he told me skating was a sport and that I would be going to secretarial school when I graduated.

I promised him I would go to secretarial school if he would let me go to the city and be in the skating meet.

I took the Greyhound bus to town and the streetcar to Mother's street. I walked down it with my skates under my arm and looked at all the house numbers. I saw that they weren't houses—they were broken-down, unpainted shacks. Little children played in the dirt outside the shacks and the stench was nauseating. I found Mother's house and saw a fire engine parked out front. Several neighbors were standing around. I wanted to turn and run but then I saw Mother.

"Nancy, darling, how are you? Come on in."

"What's happened, Mother?"

"Oh nothing. Howard had another attack. Let me look at you. Well, you're certainly getting to be a beauty."

When we walked into the house I saw Howard lying on the couch and his belly looked nine months pregnant. The firemen were doing something to him and the whole place smelled of stale beer.

"Mother, what are you doing in a place like this?"

"It's all we can afford. Howard hasn't been working and it's been very hard for us. I still have my job but I don't make enough money. But I don't want to talk about me—I want to hear about you. I hear you're quite a skater!"

"Mother, what's wrong with Howard?"

"He drank a little too much and they had to pump his stomach."

21   "Where's Jimmy?"

"He's in his bedroom. I'm glad you're here. Maybe you can talk him into going outside to play. All he does is stay in his room and draw. Howard says he's very good but that he should get out with other children."

Jimmy's room was strewn with papers and drawings. I picked them up and looked at them.

"Hey, Jimmy, they're good."

"Thanks."

When I got a good look at Jimmy I wanted to cry. He was very blond, very pale, and very skinny. I asked him why he didn't go outside more often and he just told me that he'd rather draw.

"Besides, the other boys tease me about my art."

I asked him if he wanted to come and live with us and he said, "I like Howard when he's sober. He isn't always drunk and he helps me with my art."

Mother seemed happy to have me and she was much easier to talk to than Doctor John. I simply couldn't understand why she lived with a drunk and put up with all the mess. I stayed weekends and when Howard sobered up he encouraged me about my skating and was a very warm, friendly man.

During the week, at home, I practiced on the creek and Harry became a secondary thing in my life. He was very persistent and kept calling me on the phone.

"I guess you don't have time for me any more."

"I tried to make you understand, Harry, but you wouldn't listen."

"Are you through with me, then?"

"No, I'd like to have you drive me to town next Saturday for the meet."

"Gee, I'm sorry, Nancy, but I have to clean out the barn Saturday."

"Okay. Can't you wish me luck?"

"I wish you luck and I wish to hell it was over."

When I arrived at Mother's the night before the race, Howard was drunk and in bed. He was so drunk he was urinating in a milk bottle beside the bed. I tried to ignore him and get myself in a good frame of mind. I went to bed early. I thought I was never going to be able to go to sleep so I tried to concentrate on relaxing my body but I knew that Howard was in the other room.

I was at the rink bright and early. I knew Howard wouldn't be there to see the events but I was hoping

Mother and Jimmy would show up. Mother had said that she would, but she never knew what shape Howard would be in or if she could leave him alone.

The clubhouse was full of people gathering around me to ask if I was going to win. The more they asked the more shaky I felt. My stomach just wouldn't be still. I had on my navy blue tights and my white warm-up jacket and my skates were sharpened to perfection.

As the time grew closer for the races, I went out on the ice and skated around, slowly warming up. The men's events were almost over and the announcer was telling the women to get ready. I skated over to the clean-shaven course which was laid out with red flags. The moment was upon me. I removed my jacket and one of the judges pinned a number on my white sweater. I lined up with the other girls for the eight-hundred-and-eighty-yard race. I won. I won the four-hundred-and-forty, too. All I needed to do was win the two-hundred-and-twenty and I would be the champion. We lined up again for the last race. I stooped over, waiting for the gunshot and the moment it happened the girl next to me stuck her skate in front of me. I fell and slid about fifty feet. I was so mad that I got up, and with a fury of energy passed everyone and won the race.

The screaming crowds surrounded me and the newspapermen were taking pictures. I had broken the New York State record. People asked, "Are you going to try for the Olympics?" "What are your plans now?"

I nodded yes and really didn't know what was going on. All I knew was—it felt good!

That night, I took the bus back to the country. I couldn't wait to tell Doctor John. "I won! I won, Doctor John!"

"I'm sure you performed well, but don't forget about your promise. I want you to start thinking about the school you want to go to."

Didn't he ever stop? I didn't want to go to some dumb secretarial school. How could I get away from him? I just couldn't stand him any longer.

Mother called on the phone to tell me she was very proud of me and Grandma was delighted. The next morning Grandma brought the Sunday paper and my breakfast to my bed. She laid all the newspaper pictures out in front of me and beamed.

23

The article read, "Recovering from a fall to become champion, she is rated one of the best prospects for the Olympics to come along in years."

I couldn't wait to tell Harry. He was impressed with my winning and said he would be over to take me out and celebrate. He took me to the Red Slipper Inn, one of the better roadhouses, and we drank several martinis. Afterwards he bought a bottle of liquor and drove to the lane.

I was very tipsy and happy with my success. Harry began kissing me and feeling my body. My mind was going crazy. No one had ever talked to me about sex but Doctor John had made it very clear that it was wrong. I had figured out for myself that it was all right if you were married. Mostly from what Grandma had said and the kids in school. The girls that were having sex were "easy lays," "bad girls," and usually the ones the boys talked and laughed about. I was rebellious but I still wanted to be liked by my peers.

Harry was stirring up all my sexual feelings and I loved all the heavy petting. I wasn't sure that I'd like his penis inside of me. That seemed dirty.

"Just take off your panties and I'll be very careful," Harry whispered.

I pulled back. "I'm afraid."

"There's nothing to it. You'll like it."

I thought about Doctor John again and finally told Harry that I wanted to go home. He was getting very angry with me and raced the car out of the lane.

*   *   *

Doctor John quickly forgot about my victory and started talking about graduation and business college again.

"We made a bargain—remember?"

"But they said I was good enough for the Olympics."

"No, sir, young lady!"

"Oh leave me alone! I don't know what I want to do. Can't I make any decisions for myself? I'm sixteen years old and you treat me like I was two. Maybe I don't want to go to business college. In fact I can't think of anything more boring."

"You'll do what I say until you're eighteen. I didn't pay out all that money all these years for you to ruin your life too. Do you want to end up like your mother, wallowing in filth and living with a drunken bum?"

24

"I'm not going to end up like that. Please leave me alone."

I ran to my room, crying. I felt trapped.

What was I going to do? How could I get away from him? I knew what I was doing and he didn't believe me at all.

That night, I took my skates and started walking towards the creek. I just had to be alone.

Then I saw something I'd never seen before. Ice—for miles and miles. The creek had overflowed and covered acres of land with water. The water had frozen solid, the full moon shone so bright it was like daylight, and the glass-clear ice stretched far into the woods. I quickly put my skates on and took off like a bullet. I couldn't stop. I skated faster and faster, through the woods and out into the open again. In my entire life I had never felt so free. All other things were unimportant.

I will have this night, this one time in my life to be completely alone and free, I thought, and at the same time I wanted to hug the whole world.

5

My fleeting moment of liberation that night on the ice turned into an obsession to be free. Free of Mother's problems, worrying about Jimmy, Grandma's mental illness, and Doctor John's tyranny. It was impossible for me to see that these people were human. I only saw that their way wasn't the way I wanted to run my life. I had ideas and I didn't want anyone interfering. Especially, I wouldn't wait for other people to make decisions for me. But how was I going to get free? I knew I didn't have a chance in Doctor John's house. Then there was Harry who was pulling me and prodding me into sexual action. That idea appealed to me but even then somewhere deep inside I knew that wasn't the whole answer.

If I married Harry, I could get away from Doctor John and then he couldn't boss me around. Mother would understand. I should finish high school, I guessed. But I couldn't wait until June. Harry wouldn't wait much longer, either. He'd find a girl that would do it. Harry was my only way out and it would serve Doctor John right.

I called Harry and he came to pick me up. We went to the country lane and parked. He kissed me and rubbed my breasts.

"Don't, Harry! Come on! Stop!"

"What's the matter? You've made me wait so long."

"Let's talk about it."

"What's to talk about?"

"I think the only right thing for us to do is get married. I thought a lot about it and I don't see anything else to do."

Harry pulled back, brushed his hair out of his eyes, and leaned up against the car door. "I don't think that's very sensible. I mean, getting married right away. Don't you think we ought to wait awhile—at least until you graduate?"

"No. I think we should get married as soon as possible. I just can't do it with you unless we're married."

"I don't make much money on the farm. I can't support you yet."

"We'd make out some way. We'd manage."

He took me in his arms again and I responded—passionately. He pulled his hand up and down inside my thighs and I pushed him away again. "No, I want to do it the right way. We have to get married. Don't you love me?"

Harry started the car and I started crying. "You don't love me. You just want to use me!"

Harry didn't say a word all the way home. I jumped out of his car and he called me back. "We could live on the farm," he said. "I don't think my mother would care. I'll call you."

I jumped back in the car and kissed him and kissed him. My problem was solved. I'd show everybody now.

The following weekend Harry and I drove to the city to tell Mother. She was a little surprised but very happy.

Mother was not one to be critical or to make speeches. She simply called me to her bedroom and said, "All I want you to remember is that men do one of three things: go out with other women, gamble, or drink." Of course I didn't believe her.

"Doctor John doesn't."

"He did once. He had a girlfriend—a redhead. Grandma found out about her and has never forgotten."

"Well, Harry's different. He loves me."

"I know, honey. It's always different when it's you that's in love."

"Will you tell Grandma for me?"

Mother called Grandma and Grandma relayed the message to Doctor John and he almost came through the phone. He said I was too young to get married, I was crazy like my mother, and he didn't want a damn thing to do with either one of us. Somehow Grandma talked Doctor John into coming to the wedding.

Harry's mother and father, Grandma, Doctor John, Mother, and Howard attended the simple ceremony held in a minister's home. It was the first time Doctor John had seen his own daughter in five years. He did his very best to be congenial and still hold his position as Patriarch.

Jimmy had not wanted to come.

Harry and I drove to Niagara Falls for our honeymoon. We stayed in an old hotel that didn't cost very much and when it was time to go to bed I undressed in the bathroom. Even though I knew it was legal, I felt dirty and ashamed.

I came out of the bathroom with my nightgown on and hurried to get under the covers. Harry was sitting on the edge of the bed in his shorts. I took a quick glance and turned away. He got under the covers with me and started to kiss me. I wanted to get up and run out—I'd changed my mind.

I had to go through with it now. Well, I'd just lie there and let him do what he wanted to. He kept kissing and feeling my whole body and I just couldn't relax. I wanted to but I didn't know how. He climbed on top of me and I felt his hard penis trying to penetrate my vagina.

I wished he'd hurry up.

I had no hymen because of my physical activities so when he finally got it in there was no problem with bleeding. It did hurt though and before I knew it he had ejaculated.

What was all that stuff?

I had guessed by now that it was all over and I hadn't felt any sexual pleasure at all. I didn't even know what my part of this act was supposed to be. The following morning we went to see the falls and when he tried to put his arm around me I felt like vomiting.

We stayed for two days and the second night Harry took a little bit more time for me to enjoy what I could. I still had no orgasm and I liked the closeness and love-making better than his penis inside me.

We arrived at Harry's farm on Sunday night. It was dark and when I tried to walk up the front steps I fell over someone.

"Don't mind him. That's Uncle George. He goes away and gets drunk and then comes back to work for Dad," Harry said.

The porch light came on and I got a good look at Uncle George. The big buckles on his overalls were covered with dried vomit, the front of his pants was wet with urine, and he was out cold. I swallowed hard and saw Harry's mother standing in the doorway with a pail.

"Here's your slop pail. We got no inside toilet."

We climbed the narrow stairs to our bedroom. Instead of a door there were old brown curtains hanging between our room and Harry's sister's room.

How could I have sex with Harry with his sister just three feet away? I'd just tell him I didn't feel good.

The lack of privacy didn't seem to bother Harry at all but I didn't know how I was ever going to try to get along with him in bed while his whole family was listening.

The next morning Harry took me on a tour of the farm. I was beginning to wonder why I hadn't asked him to take me there before. It was unbelievably run down. The fences were all broken down, the cows stood in a filthy barn all covered with flies, and the two work horses were suffering the same way. The house and the barns were falling apart and it was instantly clear to me that no one cared about anything. It was hard for me to believe because Harry had always looked so neat and clean.

What had I got myself into? At least I was away from Doctor John. I'd have to do the best I could. And I remembered Grandma had told me that my man was my job for life.

In the days that followed I tried to paint and fix up our bedroom, go to school every day, and keep a happy attitude. It wasn't easy. Harry's mother made it very clear that I was an outsider.

"Harry was born on this farm and he likes working with his father."

Grandma mailed me a white dress for graduation and both families showed up for the exercises. Afterwards my class went to a party but Harry and I went to a roadhouse to drink.

Drinking was a big part of our life but, unlike Doctor John, no one paid much attention because Harry and his father and uncle stayed drunk most of the time. I was beginning to drink right along with them, to ease the pain of my existence.

Mother had me meet her in town one day and took me to a doctor to get a diaphragm. By now I knew I didn't want children and I had made Harry start to use a rubber. He didn't like that much but I insisted. My mother was very matter-of-fact about birth control.

"You're too young to have children and this is a very good way of not having them. He'll measure you and show you how to use it."

Harry was pleased with the new way—he really hated rubbers.

The farm was still being neglected except for what Harry and I tried to do. I learned to milk the cows, drive the tractor, pitch hay, and feed the animals.

"I'll bet we could make this into a real nice farm, Harry."

"What's wrong with it now?"

"It's not very successful, is it?"

29   "It's okay for my folks. They like it."

"Harry, why don't you look for another job so we can move into a place of our own?"

"Yeah, someday. My folks need me right now."

"We need to be alone, Harry."

"Aren't you happy?"

"Yes, but there's better things in life—out there."

"You always did have big ideas, Nancy. Maybe it was a mistake—getting married."

"No. It's just that I don't think your mother likes me."

"That's your imagination. Come on, let's go eat."

Harry's mother had the usual dinner on the wooden table. Meat, potatoes, and bread.

I felt it was time to make my big announcement about going to the city to find a job. Harry's father paid no attention and kept pushing food into his mouth. Harry was surprised and his mother turned red.

She wiped her chin with her hand. "I think it's about time you started to think about a young one. That's the natural thing for a woman to do."

"But we don't want children yet. Do we, Harry?"

"Well, I don't know."

"Harry, we agreed. No children until we have a home of our own."

"This is your home," Harry's mother said.

I was angry. "It's your home, not ours."

I told them that it was definite. I was going to find work. Harry's mother looked stern and solemn. Things weren't going as she had planned them for Harry. I didn't really want children. I never even liked to babysit when people asked me. All I really wanted to do was live—out there.

6 A school friend told me about a company that needed help. I got up early, drove to the city, and put an application in at the plant. When I talked to the employment manager he said there was an opening in the blueprint department developing blueprints. It paid fifty dollars a week and I took the job. The company made railway signals and switches. On the way back to the farm I knew what I was eventually going to do. I had to leave Harry and I had to leave that farm.

When I pulled into the driveway Harry was holding a beautiful pinto horse. "It's for you, Nancy."

"It's gorgeous! Oh, you beautiful animal," I said, hugging its neck.

Harry put the saddle on while I changed my clothes. I jumped on and rode as fast as I could. When I returned Harry rubbed him down and put him in the barn.

"I love him," I said to Harry.

"I'm glad. Now maybe you'll stay here a while longer."

I turned away from Harry and knew at that moment that they had bought me the horse to trap me there. I told Harry I had a job and he said he was hoping I'd forget about a job and maybe stay home and have a baby. I couldn't do that and I was mixed up again. There was always a catch.

Monday morning on the new job was exciting. I developed prints for the engineers and soon came to know them all. My first paycheck made me feel independent and I put some of it in a savings account.

As time passed, I grew more and more curious about what went on in the engineering department. On my lunch hour I watched the engineers and draftsmen designing and drawing. The chief engineer showed me around and explained to me about some of the mechanical drawings.

Then I asked him if I could try drafting. In a matter of weeks I was out of the blueprint department and sitting at a drawing board—a trainee draftsman. I was the only female in the engineering department. I applied myself and my boss was a very strict teacher. One mistake and I had to do the entire drawing over. There was time, then, to do things perfectly.

When I got my first pay raise I decided to go to night school and study mechanical drawing. This meant that I rarely saw Harry, and the farm became a place to eat, sleep, and ride my horse. When I finished night school I had a set routine. I worked all day, came home, rode until dark, and had sexual intercourse only when I couldn't put Harry off any longer. I was fighting a torment inside me and I either took it out on the horse or got drunk with Harry.

"You're going to kill that horse if you don't stop riding it so hard," Harry said. "You never walk him or cool him off."

I didn't seem to care. I just rode him harder and harder. One day when I got home from work, the horse was dead. I lay on him and wept but I knew I was free to leave the farm then. I started to make a plan.

One night after everyone was asleep I sneaked downstairs with an armful of clothes. I was going to drive away and never return. Harry's mother, in a chenille robe and curlers, stood in the dark. "You're not leaving my son," she said. "Now go back to bed."

She scared me so much that I dropped all my clothes and ran back to bed. I lay in bed and thought about the mess I'd made of my life. The only thing I'd liked in the past year was my work. I wanted to run away. I had to run away. I knew it wasn't anyone's fault. Harry's people were what they were, but it wasn't enough for me. I had ambition and I wanted to find out what was out there in that big world. I wanted to go back to skating too. I was eighteen and only beginning my life. I closed my eyes, thinking if I was patient my chance would come.

It was on a Sunday afternoon, right after dinner, that the news came over the radio. The Japanese had bombed Pearl Harbor.

Our work load at the office increased immediately. Harry's mother went to the draft board several times to tell them that Harry was needed on the farm and couldn't go to war. At work everyone pitched in to do his part, but Harry didn't want to. Young men enlisted and women started to do men's jobs. Six more women came to work as draftsmen.

Every night Harry and I got drunk because if I got him drunk enough I wouldn't have to have sex with him.

It was at my drawing board that I made my decision. I went to my boss and told him I was quitting. I got my money out of the bank, called the railroad station for reservations on the train to Cleveland, left the car in the parking lot, called a cab, and left.

I boarded the train with nothing except my money and the clothes I had on my back. I watched the lights go by as the train rolled out of Rochester, New York. Jimmy had joined the Coast Guard and was in Cleveland. Maybe I could find him.

I didn't know what was ahead of me and I didn't care. I just knew that I had a glorious feeling of excitement and adventure inside me. The mess I had made would soon be gone. I knew Harry loved me but I didn't care. I didn't want to hurt Grandma but she would get over it. Mother would always understand.

The car I was riding in was full of servicemen. They smiled at me and offered me drinks out of their fifths. I moved closer and we all got roaring drunk. A soldier put his arm around me and kissed me. I put my head on his shoulder and passed out.

I had blanked out everything. The past was gone forever and there was a new life waiting.

7 I walked around in Cleveland, marveling at all the lights and all the people. I stopped at a drugstore and asked where the YWCA was. It was a very old grey building on a dark street and it looked cold. I walked up to the desk and asked if they had a room.

"Don't you have any suitcases?" the woman asked.

"My mother is sending them later."

"Well, I guess it's all right. But remember, we have strict rules here. You have to be in by eleven and no boys allowed."

My room was small, the window was small, and the decorating not very imaginative. The bathroom and showers were down the hall and when I looked out I saw other girls milling, talking, and laughing. I imagined they were laughing at me and I quickly closed the door, sat on the hard bed, and cried. Shortly I pulled myself together, grabbed a towel from the end of the bed, and headed for the showers. The bar of soap was so tiny I couldn't even work up a lather. Back in my room, I put my slip on and crawled between the disinfected-smelling sheets. In the darkness, in this strange room, I wondered if I'd done the right thing.

In the morning, I took one look at the horrible food in the cafeteria and decided to eat out. At the restaurant counter I sat next to a sailor.

"This your home town?" he asked.

"No. I just got here last night."

"Where you from?"

"I'm from Rochester, New York. I came here to work."

"I'm from Nebraska. I'm stationed here on a destroyer."

"Are you going overseas?"

"Sometime soon, I think."

I excused myself to get a paper. I turned to the want-ads.

"There's a lot of drafting jobs in the paper," I said.

"Never heard of a girl doing that kind of work," he said.

"Here's one that sounds pretty good. 'Large corporation making x-ray machines for overseas needs draftsmen.' I'm going to go there."

We finished breakfast and he offered me a cigarette.

"What's your name?"

"Nancy."

"Mine's Karl."

We walked out to the street and I noticed how tall and handsome he was. I didn't want to leave him and he didn't want to leave me. "What are you going to do now?" he asked.

"I'm going to take a taxi to the plant and apply for that job. Then I'm going to try and find a place to live. That YWCA is spooky."

"Say, could I see you again?"

"Sure. I don't know where I'll be, though."

"Can you meet me here again tomorrow morning?"

"Okay."

Karl found me a taxi. I got in, said goodbye, and watched him walk down the street, cocking his sailor hat to the back of his head.

I was hired and spent the rest of the day looking for a place to live. One ad in the paper caught my eye: "Unusual Rooms."

I took a streetcar to the address and was greeted at the door by a charming woman about forty who led me to a lovely antique-furnished living room.

"I have very nice girls living here," she said. "I have no rules. I just expect everyone to use their own judgment about things. The rent is fourteen dollars a week."

She showed me the room. It was almost like my room at Doctor John's. I took it immediately. She introduced me to Lily, the girl who had the room next to mine.

Lily said, "You'll love it here. Carol is just like a mother to all of us."

All the way to the YWCA and back I felt exhilarated. Everything was working out so great. I'd start my job on Monday. I'd see Karl in the morning, and Lily would be a good friend.

I borrowed some paper and an envelope from Lily and wrote Mother a letter asking her to try and get my clothes and to somehow see about getting me a divorce from Harry. I knew she would understand.

When the letter was written I went back to Lily's room and we talked. She had been home from work for a week because she wasn't feeling well. Lily was tall, blonde, and a little heavy and we felt close right from the beginning. She told me that she wrote to her boyfriend, who was in the Army, almost every day. They were to be married when he got home.

"Most of the girls in the house are waiting for someone. It's so hard waiting, and waiting."

I told her all about Harry and why I'd left him. "I sure don't want to get into another mess like that," I said.

My bed was soft and comfortable and I could hear music coming from Lily's radio. Everything was all right so far and I went to sleep thinking about seeing Karl in the morning.

He was sitting in the restaurant when I got there and we ate breakfast. I gave him my new address and phone number and told him all about my new job and the place I'd found to live.

I was in love. Karl and I spent all the time together that we could. We swam, drank, danced, and made love. He was everything I'd always dreamed about. Handsome, strong, and masculine. I liked having sex with him but still didn't have an orgasm. I was learning how to have sex though and even if I only thought I was pleasing him it was all right. If I reflect, I realize that part of my love was his uniform. War is very seductive.

Together we drank more and more. We found a favorite bar where all the servicemen and girls hung out and spent most of our spare time there. I was beginning to sleep late and was waking up with terrible hangovers. My boss was very upset and warned me several times. I complained bitterly to Karl.

"He gives me a pain. I think I'll look for another job."

"Whatever you think is best, honey. I have some bad news too. We're going out on sea trials and I don't know whether we're coming back here or not."

I blew up. "You can't do that! You can't leave me now!"

"I don't want to, but the Navy comes first."

"My mother sent my divorce papers, too. Some friend of Howard's testified that he had intercourse with me. That's the only way you can get a divorce in New York. We could get married now. Damn that Navy!"

"Will you wait for me?"

"Of course I'll wait for you. I love you."

39   "We'll get married when I get back."

I hugged and squeezed him and cried.

Karl's ship was leaving the next morning and the captain had told his men that the wives and girlfriends could come to the pier to say goodbye. I didn't even bother to go to work. I just put on my blue dress, black trench coat, and tam, and walked downtown to the pier. Karl came toward me, hugged me very tight, and then kissed me. That was the moment I realized that he really was going away. I've always had a hard time with reality. Karl asked me again if I would wait and I promised I would. When I looked around I got scared. The whole scene was like a nightmare.

Men, women, and children were milling everywhere; some laughing, some crying, some children clinging to their dads' pant legs, and some dads were throwing their children up in the air. I could hardly hold back the tears.

After Karl boarded his ship, I walked back to the main street feeling sick inside. An Armistice Day parade was in progress. Hundreds of flags were flying. Soldiers, sailors, and marines were marching to the blare of their bands. People lined the sidewalks. I stared at everything trying to sift things through my mind. Some people were alone, some were not. How many of these people were the lonely ones like me? Suddenly I wanted to scream, "Stop! Stop marching!"

I walked faster and faster, with my hands over my ears, until I saw a sign, "Cocktails." I ran in and sat down at the bar. I ordered a martini. The hurt was gone.

8

I was tired of my boss calling me into his office to warn me about being late. All he cared about was the work. I finally quit and found another job with the Army Engineers. Although it paid more money, I still had a hard time getting up in the mornings. I spent all of my free time sitting in a bar, drinking and talking to servicemen. Everything they were doing seemed so exciting.

At work we were drawing maps and I was drawing contour lines. It took an hour every morning for my hands to stop shaking so I could do my work without botching it up. I really didn't want to work. I wanted to play. No one in the office knew what our work was about and I didn't find out until much later. We were drawing maps of Hiroshima and Nagasaki.

Sunday afternoon was the only time I stayed home. Lily and I bought beer and listened to classical music on her radio.

"Damn, I wish Karl would come back. I know they've gone overseas. I should be getting a letter soon. Don't you get tired of waiting, Lily?"

"Yes, I do. But Karl's in the Navy and that's different. He'll be back sooner than Frank. I try to write every day but I can't think of anything to say."

"I couldn't wait long for Karl. I'd go out of my mind."

Lily bent over and held her belly.

"What's the matter?"

"I don't know. It's that pain again."

"Are you sick again? I'm worried about you. You don't look too good lately. You're awful thin."

"I'm okay now. I'll be all right."

"Do you want to go to the bar and have a real drink?"

"Let's do that."

We sat at the bar, ordered drinks, and looked around. Nothing had changed. The place was packed with servicemen. The jukebox blared, "Don't sit under the apple tree with anyone else but me," and the girls were hugging, laughing, dancing, and drinking with the boys in uniform.

"Same old thing," Lily said.

"Sometimes I wonder how many girls would be in here if all the boys were in civilian clothes."

"I never thought about it."

"The first time I saw Karl in his uniform I just about died. He was beautiful."

41 "Have you ever seen him in civvies?"

"No. Gee, Lily, you're taking all the romance out of it."

Two Air Force lieutenants started talking to us and then ordered us drinks. I was getting bored with the bar scene and didn't pay too much attention. All I really wanted to do was drink. Lily had struck up a conversation with one of them and the other started talking to me.

"My name's Joe. What's yours?"

"Nancy, and I'm not in the mood to talk."

"Okay."

He didn't try to find someone else to talk to. He just sat next to me, silent. I took quick glances at him and picked up another drink. He wasn't exceptional. He just looked like all the other servicemen. He just kept sitting there. I spoke first.

"You've been overseas?"

"Several times."

"I wish the war would end."

"Me too."

He didn't seem to expect anything from me so I kept up the conversation, feeling rather at ease. We talked for a while and then Lily said she was going home with the other officer. Joe and I stayed. After several more drinks I was pretty tipsy and he walked me home. I gave him my phone number. Lily was already in when I got home.

"How'd you like the guy you were with?" I asked Lily.

"He was okay."

"I gave Joe my phone number."

"Are you going out with him?"

"I don't know, Lily. All I know is that I'm sick of waiting for Karl. I haven't heard from him and I don't even remember what he looks like. Joe's a Flying Tiger, you know."

We said good night and went to bed.

It was about three when I heard Lily scream and I ran to her room.

"What's wrong, Lily? Lily? Lily? What's the matter?"

"No! No! I don't want anyone to know."

"Know what? Lily, I have to do something."

"I had an abortion. Something went wrong. I don't want Frank or my parents to know. Frank thinks I've been faithful to him. Oh, I can't stand the pain!"

I ran and got Carol and she called a doctor. They

rushed Lily to the hospital. After the operation Lily went home to her parents for a month. I felt lost again.

It was two weeks before Joe called and then he took me to dinner at the Statler Hotel. It was nothing like the bars and lounges I'd been hanging around. The music was soft and the food excellent. We danced and Joe held me close. I felt relaxed for the first time in months. He took me home fairly early. Somehow Joe made me feel at ease and very womanly. But it made me angry that he didn't drink very much.

He took me to the horseraces and I had fun. On the way home he said he wanted to stop by his apartment a minute. The apartment was lovely and he shared it with two other officers. There was no one home but he made no attempt to seduce me. I was more and more confused about my feelings because I thought I loved Karl. But Joe was someone special—mature, gentle, and, even with all the battle ribbons running down his chest, tender. He refused to talk about the war and had an attitude of quiet acceptance.

He sure was different. Not really handsome, but he seemed so strong—inside or somewhere.

All the men I'd met talked about the war, telling truths and untruths, depending on the situation. Sometimes they told it dramatically for pity and sometimes with affection, as though it were a great love affair. Joe baffled me.

"Do you want to stay for supper or do you want to go home?" Joe asked.

"I'd like to stay."

Together we fixed steak and all the trimmings. The other two officers came home. We all had drinks and ate. They were very impressed when I told them what my job was.

Joe took me home, stood at the front door with me, and told me he'd had a wonderful time. I wondered if he was ever going to kiss me. He finally pulled me gently to him and put his lips to mine. There was no flash of lights turning on. It was simply nice.

I received a letter from Karl telling me his ship wouldn't be back for a while and that he loved me and knew I was waiting. I was all mixed up again. I had promised Karl I would wait and I was going out with Joe. Joe never asked anything of me and I was feeling closer and

43

closer to him all the time. He let me be myself and a woman. I wanted to go to bed with him but I thought I should be true to Karl. It still annoyed me that Joe would only drink one or two drinks during an evening and when I came home from a date with him, I drank in my room alone until I passed out.

Suddenly I stopped hearing from him. His silence went on for two weeks. I was heartbroken and in desperation drank more and more during my lunch hour, after work, and in the evenings. I wasn't eating properly either.

One morning when the alarm rang, I jumped out of bed and fell flat on the floor. I couldn't get up or move. I was completely paralyzed.

"Carol, Carol!" I screamed.

Carol came and immediately called her doctor. I didn't have to go to the hospital but I did have to stay in bed. The doctor said I was in a very run-down condition and gave me a shot. I was able to move again but my whole body felt weak and I was afraid to ask the doctor what was wrong. I knew.

Carol fixed meals for me and Lily returned to our boarding house well but thinner than she had been. I was so glad to see her.

Finally, Joe called. He came to visit me and it was the happiest moment I'd had in weeks. When I had recovered sufficiently he took me out to dinner again.

"I'll have a martini," I said.

"No, I'm not going to buy you a martini," Joe calmly said.

"Why?"

"I've wanted to tell you something for a long time and I hope it doesn't hurt your feelings. Nancy, I love you very much and I'd like to marry you some day when the war is over, but you're in trouble with your drinking."

"Oh, Joe, do you mean that? We'll have to have a drink to celebrate!"

"I don't think you heard me, Nancy. From now on you'll have to buy your own drinks. I can't stop you."

"Everybody drinks, Joe. I don't drink any more than anyone else."

"You were just sick. Do you know what was wrong?"

"Yes. I had the flu."

"I talked to the doctor. You had alcoholic paralysis."

"That's nonsense. I don't drink that much and besides I can stop any time I want to."

"Okay. Then you don't have to drink tonight, do you?"

"No. No. I don't."

The rest of the evening was difficult because I had nothing to falsify my inadequate feelings. I was in a position where Joe made all the decisions. He drove to his apartment, turned on soft music, and took me in his arms again, tenderly. He asked me if I wanted to sleep with him and I was afraid and full of old guilts. It had been years since I had had sex without any alcohol first.

I wanted to, but I didn't even know how without a drink. Oh God, this was all wrong. Something was all wrong.

It wasn't. Joe held me and rubbed my back gently. He never once put his hand on my breasts or parts that he thought I didn't want him to touch. He kissed me again. I relaxed and walked to his bed. This moment was more beautiful than I had ever imagined. Drinking was gone from my mind. Joe and I were one. I had the first orgasm I'd ever had and I never wanted to leave him—ever.

Our moments in bed together were, from then on, the very best experiences of my entire life. I stopped drinking so much, worked, played, and had a glorious time.

I couldn't believe it when Joe told me he had to go back overseas. If ever I had a chance for a halfway normal life it was then.

"I'm going to worry about you," Joe said.

"You've been over there enough times. Why won't they let you stay here?"

"Nancy, I've been ordered to go."

"Who does all this anyway? How many times do they expect you to go?"

"As many times as I'm needed."

I hung onto him. "I won't let you go."

"Come on, Nancy. It'll all be over soon."

I saw red. "I hate this goddamn war."

"You're not the only woman who's being left behind. Many have waited for three years. Or more."

"Isn't that lovely? And who gives a damn about them? And the widows? What do they get? Stupid medals? Well, you can't go to bed with a medal!"

I cried and Joe comforted me. "I love you, Nancy. Always remember that."

I got one letter from Joe. The next one was from his roommate. Joe had been killed on a mission.

9 A sailor was playing the organ. I was dressed in a steel-grey suit, white gloves, and white hat. Karl stood beside me in his blue uniform. A chaplain was performing the ceremony. I had traveled to Norfolk, Virginia. It was April 1945.

My loneliness had been unbearable and my constant drinking was the only thing that deadened the hurt. When Karl wired me to come to Norfolk to get married, I saw a way out of my predicament.

He loved me and I'd make him such a good wife that he'd accept my baby too. But I wouldn't tell him until after we were married. Dear God, I had to have a father for my baby. What would people think?

After the wedding we went to the hotel where Karl had reserved a suite and it seemed as though a hundred sailors came to congratulate us and get completely drunk. Champagne was everywhere and Karl and I proceeded to get just as drunk as everyone else.

It was very early in the morning when the last sailor left. We decided to call our mothers. After blubbering and crying into the phone we both passed out.

In the morning Karl ordered breakfast in the room.

"Guess I really goofed last night," he said.

"So did I."

"Well, I won't this morning," he said, reaching for me. I had learned much from Joe so I made sure that I was satisfied with Karl.

Somehow it wasn't the same.

Afterwards I put my hand on his chest. "There's something I want to tell you, Karl."

"What, honey?"

"It was awful while you were gone. I got so lonesome. Please don't get mad at me, but I'm three months pregnant."

Karl jumped up out of bed and began throwing things as fast as he could. I never saw him so angry and it frightened me. He put on his clothes and ran out the door. Hours went by and I drank all the champagne that was left from the party and fell back into a chair.

Why didn't he come back? I was so scared. Would he ever come back? God, what had I done?

The door opened and Karl came in.

"I've thought it all out. There's nothing much we can do about it now. We'll just have to live with it somehow.

And don't ever tell me who it was, because I don't want to know one thing more about it. Do you understand that?"

When the money ran out we had to find a cheaper place to live. Karl made only sixty-four dollars a month but he did have plans for being promoted. He looked in the newspaper and found a room for rent—the cheapest one—for fourteen dollars a week. We rode the streetcar for several miles. It was so hard to find a place to live that you had to get there right away or lose it.

The room was in an attic and we crawled up a ladder and through a hole to get to it. Karl was so tall that he couldn't stand up straight—the rafters were in his way. One iron cot and one army cot were pushed together to make a double bed and one was about an inch higher than the other. The only place to wash was a sink in the corner and we were going to have to go to the second floor to take a bath or use the toilet. We took the room.

In the months that followed we moved several times and in one place the landlady showed me how to start knitting a baby blanket. I'd never done anything like that in my life and I liked it.

One day the landlady and her husband called Karl and me downstairs.

"Do you kids hear all the noise?"

"Yes, I hear it now," I answered.

Bells, horns you toot, car horns, and church chimes.

"The war in Europe is over," the landlady proclaimed.

"Oh wow!" I hugged and kissed Karl.

Her husband poured us all drinks to celebrate victory.

Now I'd have Karl forever. I was so sick of men going to war and it was over.

It wasn't long before the power of the atomic bomb was unleashed on Hiroshima and Nagasaki and that ended all of World War Two. Peace had come at last—to the whole world.

*　　*　　*

The time was near for my baby to arrive and we had to find a more suitable place than one room. We found an apartment and at the same time Karl was promoted to first class. This meant more money and we needed all the money we could get. Rents were too high and Navy pay was too low. The waiting lists for Navy housing were so long that it would take a year to get in.

48

The new apartment was actually the upstairs of a big house. It had a small kitchen, a large bedroom, and a living room with a potbellied stove. The coal pile was in the backyard and Karl carried the buckets of coal up the stairs to keep us warm.

I fixed things up with what little I had to work with and felt good about our first real home.

"We're going out to sea for five days. Will you be all right?"

"That's not too long. I'm sure the baby won't come until you get back. At least I hope not."

"If it does, just call the hospital and they'll send an ambulance."

I had been going to the Navy hospital for my check-ups and found them so busy that I had to sit and wait for hours.

Karl left me the next morning and I was alone for the first time since I got married. It was October and cold. That afternoon I carried a bucket of coal up the long flight of stairs and that night I fell into a deep sleep. About two I woke with a start. My water had broken.

Oh my God! What was I going to do?

I went to the bathroom and put a towel between my legs. My whole body trembled as I walked down the long stairs and to the house across the street. I knocked and a grandmother-type woman came to the door.

"I think I'm going to have a baby."

"Oh, my dear, come in, come in."

"I can't. My water broke and I'll ruin your carpeting. Would you please call the Navy hospital?"

"Yes, yes, I'll call right away and I'll get my daughter to go home with you."

In a moment the daughter came to the door in her nightgown and robe. "I'll wait with you until the ambulance comes."

I didn't climb the stairs. I sat on the porch. The girl got my suitcase for me and in minutes the hospital corpsmen were lifting me into the ambulance.

I was in hard labor for twenty-four hours and the pain was so terrible I thought I was dying. I hollered for Karl and screamed at everyone. No one had ever told me how bad it hurt to have a baby.

Chris was born October 29, 1945. Karl arrived home and he and his buddy came to the hospital, drunk, to see the baby and me. He leaned over and gave me a quick kiss on the cheek.

I was glad he was drunk so he wouldn't be able to say anything to me about Chris not being his baby.

"Did you bring me a drink?"

"Didn't think about it. Hey, Frankie, let's go to the nursery and take a look at my son."

It seemed strange to have another human life to take care of. I did it mostly by guesswork, having had no experience at all. I did have feelings of love for my baby and I knew he was mine and mine alone. No one could take that away.

When Chris was a few weeks old Karl invited sailors and their girlfriends to our house for a party. I was happy to have drinks around again and everyone proceeded to get very drunk. It was late when they all left and Karl was getting mean.

"You're pretty drunk, Karl. Why don't you go to bed?"

"How can you just sit there, stupid? How the hell do you think I've felt the last six months? Now I gotta raise someone else's kid."

"Karl, don't say these things to me, please. You said it was all right. That you'd try."

"Shut up, slut. How the hell many guys did you lay with anyway?"

"Come on, let's go to bed."

"Leave me alone, goddamn it! I think I'll go out and find me someone. Why not?"

"Please, Karl!"

I gently took his arm. He slapped my face and left.

It was dawn when he came back and he looked terrible. I got up and fixed a baby bottle while Karl changed into his uniform. He said he'd eat breakfast on the ship.

* * *

In the spring of 1946 Karl was transferred to Orange, Texas. His ship was going to be decommissioned and he told me he'd send for me as soon as he found a place for us to live. He was promoted to chief petty officer and my allotment check was raised to a hundred-and-eighty dollars. I had tried to make up to Karl for my mistake and keep some sort of a home. I guess I would have done anything to make him forget that Chris was not his. However, he seemed happiest when we were partying and all his buddies were around.

When Karl left, I felt lost and lonely again. I played with Chris, took him for walks in a carriage a neighbor had given me, window-shopped, and went back to an empty apartment. I wouldn't even consider going out at night because Norfolk was jammed with sailors. Every street in town was a sea of white hats.

Occasionally I bought a six-pack of beer and drank it in the evenings. I had no friends, no relatives, and knew only one neighbor—the woman across the street who had called the ambulance and given me the carriage.

The letters from Karl were nice but he never mentioned anything about finding a place to live and sending for me.

Chris was five months old when I decided I was sick of being alone. I made arrangements for the Navy to pick up my household effects, and bought a plane ticket for Texas. I didn't tell Karl I was coming.

I wore the grey suit I was married in and Chris had diarrhea all the way to Texas. It came out of the disposable diaper onto my lap and the stewardess had to come to my rescue. I wanted to cry.

When I arrived in Beaumont I had to take a taxi to Orange and the fare was fifteen dollars. I went directly to the pier and found that Karl's ship was anchored out in the water. They sent word to him and a small boat brought him in.

"What are you doing here?"

"I wanted to be with you."

"I don't know where we're going to live. I told you to wait."

"Wait? I waited. Aren't you glad to see me?"

"You could have told me you were coming but I am glad to see you."

Karl kissed me and told me that we could stay with another sailor and his wife until we found a place of our own. I was so exhausted from lugging Chris that I would have slept on the ground.

Karl was able to get us into Federal housing. It was all that was available and all we could afford. Our unit was in the middle of a row of several attached shacks.

The one couch and one chair had wooden arms and worn-out leather cushions. The pots and pans were corroded from so many people using them and the dishes were cracked and chipped. The floors were old wood and bare. I walked around inspecting everything, and immediately started thinking of ways I could fix it up.

"Karl, come quick! Look at those bugs! What in the world are they?"

Inside the shower there were about ten two-inch bugs.

"They look like cockroaches," Karl said.

"Well, get rid of them, whatever they are."

Karl inspected them again. "They are cockroaches!"

"I guess it's true—everything in Texas is *big!*"

Karl found a spray can under the sink and killed the roaches. He picked up a dead one and ran after me with it. I fell on the bed and Karl kissed me. Chris was asleep.

10

I made curtains out of Navy bedspreads, cleaned and scrubbed, and covered the dirty furniture with sheets. A heavy Navy swab came with the house and strands from it clung to the spintery floor. It was difficult to keep the place clean because the entire housing project was surrounded with dirt.

The two-hundred-and-fifty-pound woman who lived across the street from me and had ten kids, knew how to clean her shack. She took a bucket of water and threw it on her floors and swept it all out her front door. That was the end of her housework. After that she propped herself up in a chair out in front of her shack and breast-fed her year-old baby. She never wore anything under her housedress and didn't seem to care. She was beautiful.

I looked at her often and wondered why my milk had dried up after trying to breast-feed Chris. The doctor said I was too nervous and that the modern way was to bottle-feed. I was trying to be a good mother and good wife. Maybe I wanted to be that to show my mother it could be done. I don't know.

My brother Jimmy was home from overseas and decided to pay us a visit. I was really surprised to see him. It had been a long time.

The day Jimmy arrived, Karl was on the ship and I talked Jimmy into getting us a bottle of whiskey. We drank fast and talked fast.

Jimmy said, "I stopped in Galveston to see what I could find out about our father."

"And?"

"He's dead."

My heart pounded. "Oh, no! And I was so close! How long ago?"

"About two months ago."

"And I could have seen him!"

"I don't think you would have wanted to. He died from alcoholism."

I took another drink. By the time Karl got home Jimmy and I were stoned. Jimmy was frying himself an egg. Karl was furious. "What's going on here?"

"I want you to meet my brother Jimmy."

"Hello. Where's Chris?"

"He's okay. He's playing in the playpen. Get out of the way, Jimmy, I'm trying to make spaghetti."

"I'm hungry now, damn it," Jimmy said.

"Looks like you two are ahead of me," Karl said, taking a big drink.

"Get out of the way, Jimmy," I screamed.

I pushed him away from the stove and he pushed me back.

"Hey, cut it out," Karl said.

I scratched Jimmy's face and he hit me again, hard.

Karl hit Jimmy and knocked him through the paper-thin wall.

"You're not going to hurt her and get away with it," Karl said.

"Your wife and my darling sister just scratched the hell out of me," Jimmy yelled.

Karl pushed him out the front door and during the scuffle Jimmy grabbed the only thing he'd brought with him, his portable radio. He stood outside the door and yelled, "Good luck, sucker. That isn't the first time I've seen her hit and scratch. She did the same thing to Harry when she was drunk. She's a cat, that one!"

"Get going, Jimmy, and don't come back."

"How dare you kick my brother out?"

"What the hell's the matter with you?"

"He's my brother, that's what."

"I don't care. He's not coming into my house and getting you drunk."

"I'm not drunk."

"Ha!"

Karl went to the bedroom and got Chris out of the playpen. "Are you going to feed him or not?"

"Of course I'm going to feed him and you if you'll just wait a few minutes. That's all you think about is food!"

I staggered around getting the food on the table and mumbling. Karl fed Chris and put him to bed.

Karl had put our name on the list for Navy housing and in three months we were able to move. The new house was better than any place we'd lived. It was a single stucco house, white with green trim, and a lawn. It was unfurnished so we went to Sears and bought the cheapest furniture we could—on credit. I was really happy, knowing that I could really have things the way I wanted them and I loved the cheap furniture.

The first night in our new house, Karl invited all his

friends from the ship for a housewarming party. They brought in cases of beer and bottles of liquor. I put Chris to bed and found a corner to sit in to drink and talk to another Navy wife. I asked her how long she'd been in the Navy.

"Fifteen years."

"Do you like it?"

"Sometimes it's all right and sometimes it's not."

"I'm really happy with our house. That Federal housing was like living in the slums."

"I know. I've lived in places like that."

Suddenly everyone started to yell, "Fire! Fire!"

I jumped up and saw smoke coming from the new Sears couch. "My God, it's my new couch!"

I watched while sailors poured beer down the smoldering hole in the couch. They laughed and laughed.

When I got up the next morning and looked at the couch, I wanted to cry. Then I heard a knock on the front door.

"Hey, anyone home?"

"Sure. Come on in."

It was the Navy wife I had talked to at the party, and she was carrying a six-pack under her arm. She seemed to be in a very cheerful mood.

"Let's have a beer."

"This early in the morning?"

"After a while you'll find it's the only thing that helps."

"Is it going to help me forget I'm pregnant?"

"Wow! Then you really need a drink."

We sat at the kitchen table and drank. It was the first time I'd ever drunk in the morning. I took another sip, looked out the front door to check Chris, sat back, relaxed, and felt that all was right with the world again.

11 I brought Mary home from the hospital and put her in the crib. I stood there smiling and at the same time tears filled my eyes.

She was beautiful. Maybe now Karl would be easier to get along with, knowing that this was his child.

Chris was two and a healthy, robust, active boy. Karl was never angry at Chris. In fact he seemed to love him very much. He threw him up in the air, taught him how to stand on Karl's hands, and absolutely thought it was great when Chris jumped off the top of a car to the ground.

"Nothing scares him," Karl said.

No one ever knew that Chris was not Karl's child.

Mary was an easy baby to take care of. She seemed much more contented than Chris ever did. But then again I had had some experience by the time she was born.

Karl received transfer orders to a destroyer in Newport, Rhode Island.

Except for the children, our life in Texas had been drinking, fighting, trying to pay bills, and trying to keep cool. The Navy pay wasn't enough for either of us to drink and try to take care of a family but I still managed to get my beer every day with the grocery money. Karl spent much of his time at the Chief's Club and whenever we were pressed by bill collectors, he borrowed money from his buddies.

When Karl told me we were being transferred, I was very excited.

When we got away from that heat, the people, and the Chief's Club, we would be all right.

We drove cross-country in a jammed-full 1940 Chrysler. In Newport we rented a nice house and immediately discovered we couldn't afford it. The rent was always too high in Navy towns but we thought we could manage—until the heating bill came. The furnace wasn't working right and our oil bill for one month was fifty dollars. We complained to the landlord and he said there was nothing he could do. When we looked for another place, there was nothing available.

We didn't have the money to drink much and for the first time since we'd been married I felt as though we might make it. Karl loved Mary and Chris and spent time in the basement making them toys. Somehow we even managed to get them a mongrel dog, black-and-white spotted and twice as long as she was tall. We named her Hedy Lamarr in honor of my idol.

I continued to crave alcohol and found it difficult to live in reality. I felt a need to escape, especially when I found out I was pregnant.

Karl took me to the Navy hospital for prenatal check-ups. Going to the Navy hospital, like going to the Navy commissary to buy groceries, meant hours and hours of waiting. Navy hospitals always made me feel as though I was only one in a herd of cattle being processed. When I complained to Karl he always answered, "This is part of our benefits and you should be grateful."

Oh yes, I should be grateful that a different doctor gives me a pelvic exam every time. So many different gods running around me.

Tim was born June 13, 1950, and when I came home Karl and I got drunk. Then Karl told me they were going out on sea trials again, for just a few days. It frightened me to be alone with three children so I was glad it was to be only a few days.

He didn't come back when he was supposed to and shortly after June 27, 1950, I received a letter:

Dear Nancy:

We are on our way to the west coast. We don't know where we're going, but no doubt by now you have heard about the war in Korea. Take care of everything and write. From now on our home port will be San Diego.

Love, Karl

I fell back on the couch, with the patched hole in it, and wept. I was really frightened. I knew no one and had no one to talk to.

Oh, no! Not again!

The children came running in. "What's wrong, Mommy?"

I tried to pull myself together. "Daddy's had to go far away. Come on, we're going to the store."

I picked up Tim from the bassinet, piled all the children into the car, and drove to the store—to get a fifth of liquor.

The days and the weeks, went by and I stayed half drunk most of the time.

One night the wind began to blow. It blew harder and faster and I didn't know what was happening. A neighbor man brought me two candles. "You might need these. We're having a hurricane. You'd better move yourself and your children to the middle of the room."

I thanked him and when he left I moved the couch to the middle of the living room and put Chris and Mary to sleep on it. I put Tim's bassinet on a chair next to the couch and when the wind got stronger, I huddled on the floor next to them. The lights went off. I got up, lit a candle, and looked out the window. The trees were bent clear down to the ground as though they were surrendering to God. Off in the distance, near the Vanderbilt mansion, I could see the watchman's lantern swinging back and forth.

Chris woke up. "What is it, Mommy?"

"It's just a bad storm, Chris. It'll be over soon." I patted him on the back and when he was asleep I poured myself a drink.

In the morning the sun came out and everything was calm. It was then that I made my decision.

I had to leave there. I couldn't stay there any longer. There was nothing for me there and if Karl's ship pulled into San Diego, I wanted to be there.

I began to make plans. I traded the old Chrysler in for a 1948 Chevrolet; no down payment, just the old car and monthly payments. I said to the salesman,"This car better get me to California or I'll park it on the side of the road and never pay for it."

He was shocked. "You don't mean that you're going to drive by yourself to California."

"Yes, I do mean it and I mean it about the car, too."

"Well, you better let me take it back in the shop and have it double-checked."

I had to wait for my allotment to come and the Navy to pick up my household belongings. The neighbor man tried to talk me out of it. "You can't drive all that way with two children and a tiny baby."

"Yes, I can and I'm going to. I'm going to be in San Diego when my husband's ship comes back."

"Who are you going to stay with?"

"I know some people in Anaheim. A guy who used to be on my husband's ship."

58   He just walked away, shaking his head.

The night before the trip I got one more bottle of liquor and got very drunk. I was aware that I couldn't drink while driving and that I was fully responsible for getting all of us across the United States safely.

I planned on making my first stop at Lily's house in Tennessee. She had married Frank, the sweetheart she'd waited for, and they lived in a small town.

Tim was nine weeks old and on a formula. I mixed it and put it in a quart thermos bottle. After my disastrous plane trip with Chris, I vowed never to use disposable diapers again and I packed four dozen cloth diapers in a separate and easily accessible suitcase. I had a small round hotplate and a pan to boil water in for the formula. I bought a case of canned milk and dextrose to complete all the ingredients needed.

Chris was four and Mary two. I furnished them with coloring books, crayons, cookies, and crackers. The neighbor man tied all my luggage on top of the car and I put Tim's bassinet lengthwise on the front seat next to me. I gave the house key back to the landlord, while the neighbor man pleaded with me to change my mind.

"I wish you'd reconsider."

"Everything's okay. We're going to make it," I assured him.

I had a full tank of gas, a gasoline credit card, and my one-hundred-and-eighty-dollar allotment check.

I was starting the car when Chris yelled, "Mommy, Mommy! Hedy!"

Mary began to cry. Hedy was sitting on the porch looking bewildered. She was also very pregnant.

I hesitated and then opened the car door and called her to get in. The fat, out-of-shape mongrel curled up on the floor of the back seat and quickly put her head down as if to say, "See, I really won't be any trouble."

I waved goodbye to my neighbor friend, who was still shaking his head, and drove off.

At the edge of Newport rain started to pour down and the wind started blowing furiously. About twenty miles out of town all the luggage blew off the top of the car. I pulled off the road, got out, and tried to rescue my suitcases. The children were very noisy and they were making me nervous. A man pulled alongside. "Having trouble, lady?"

59   "Yes, I am. I guess my things weren't tied very tight."

I could barely stand up with the wind blowing so hard so the man got out to help me.

"Well, with all this rain and no tarp we'd better see if we can fit it in your trunk and back seat."

He got some of it in the trunk of the car and then opened the car door to put a huge foot locker on the floor.

"Well, two little ones and a dog, eh?"

I had to do something so I told him to go ahead and fit it in. The dog could sleep on top or curl up smaller beside it.

"Where you headed?"

"California."

"California? You're kidding?"

"Nope."

"With two kids and a dog?"

"Nope. With three kids and a dog. There's another one in the front seat."

The man peered in the window. "Well, I'll be damned. A baby! Do you really think you're doing the right thing?"

"I know I am if I can just get going."

"Well, lady, all I can say is, good luck."

I started the car. "I really appreciate your help. Thanks."

"That's okay. Just be careful—please."

I waved and drove off again.

I drove only ninety miles the first day and when I stopped at a motel I was very disgusted at the bad weather and my bad luck.

I bought hamburgers for Chris, Mary, and me, fixed Tim's formula with the hotplate, washed out some diapers, and tucked the children into bed. They went right to sleep and I crawled into my bed.

Why was I so nervous? I hoped no one would break in. I was glad I'd brought the dog—she was some protection. If I just had a drink. No. I couldn't do that. Tomorrow I'd do better. I had to relax. Relax your body. Think of something pleasant. What was that noise? God, I was nervous. Maybe I really was doing the wrong thing. No, it was too late. I had to go on.

It seemed forever before I dozed off but I had made new plans for the following night. The next day I drove about two hundred and fifty miles and I felt better. Before I stopped at a motel, I found a liquor store, quickly ran in, and bought a half-pint. After going through the same ritual as the night before, plus bathing the children, I drank the whole bottle and fell asleep.

In the morning my mouth was extremely dry but I knew I'd have to clip off a few hundred miles before getting my much-needed reward.

I drove into New York City and out again across the George Washington Bridge. I lost my way several times. The confusion almost made me wish I'd never started and the children, of course, picked that particular time to fight. My nerves were jumping out of my body but I was soon out and on the highway again.

Every morning I was thirsty and every night I bought a half-pint. People were so helpful. Neighbors in the motels would go out and get food for us. Everybody offered to help me. Total strangers.

I got through Washington, D.C., and the Great Smoky Mountains. The heavily wooded slopes, disguising themselves with a blue-grey haze, made me think of heaven.

I found Lily's house, several miles out of Knoxville, in the country. We hugged and kissed each other and then she introduced me to her husband, Frank. He owned and operated a small garage and gas station and immediately took my car to check it over. Lily and I took the children into the house.

Lily and Frank had no children.

Hedy was out running around the fields glad for the exercise and then she hid under Lily's house. All the coaxing in the world couldn't get her out.

Mary and Chris played outside and Tim slept in his bassinet.

"How about a beer?"

"I thought you'd never ask," I said.

"Frank and I never had any children because of the abortion. I had to have a complete hysterectomy. He loves kids and telling him was the hardest thing I ever had to do. But we're here, settled and happy."

We stayed several more days with Lily and when Hedy finally came out from underneath the house she was very thin.

12

I was prepared to leave Hedy and her puppies at Lily's until we got in the car. Then Mary and Chris begged and pleaded with me to take them along. I tried to talk them out of it but it was no use. We put the seven puppies on the floor of the car and Hedy jumped in with them.

I thanked Lily and Frank for all their help and we were on the road again.

I taught Mary and Chris to sing "California, Here I Come," and I was certain now I was going to make it. Not many people I met were sure—but I was.

Gas station attendants asked where I was going and when I told them, they didn't believe me. Some told me to turn around and go back. I laughed and kept right on going. I drove through rain storms, sleet storms, and temperature changes. I was driving more miles every day and going through the same routine every night. Making formula, washing diapers, feeding the kids and Hedy, and finally at the end—my half-pint.

People in the motels were fantastic, fussing over the children and offering help. No one took advantage of me. They just showed me warmth and friendship. The strength I got from all the people gave me the courage I needed. Life took on a new meaning—I feared no one.

Every state had a uniqueness of its own and its own particular beauty. In Oklahoma City I picked up Route 66.

Texas was spacious and rainy and the children were beginning to get on my nerves. Mary insisted on playing with the newborn pups and I constantly had to yell at her. Chris helped some in trying to keep her from touching them but every once in a while Hedy would let out a low growl. Once I had to stop the car and let the children out to play.

When I started out again, Mary was back at the puppies again and I screamed, "If you don't leave those puppies alone I'm going to throw them out the window."

That worked for a while.

I didn't want to make any extra stops because I had been stopping every four hours to fill the baby bottle with formula from the thermos. I drove the car with my left hand and fed Tim with my right hand.

Life, new life all around me. My babies and new puppies and I was responsible for getting them somewhere safe. If I could just have a drink. I was really getting nervous—it's a long way across that desert. I had to make sure I had enough water. I hoped nothing went wrong with the car. So far, so good. I'd have to have the oil checked at the next stop. A radio in the car would have helped some but I couldn't afford that. Oh God, let me make it, please, I prayed.

The Indians along the highway in New Mexico fascinated Chris and me. Mary was too young to appreciate them. I felt a great sadness, for some reason. I guess I'd never thought much about Indians.

I had spent seven days on the road—a long time for some people but I knew I'd made good time. I was in Arizona, the last state before California.

Suddenly I saw the Painted Desert. I stopped the car and we got out to look. I was speechless.

"Mommy, look at all the colors!" Chris exclaimed.

"I see them, Chris."

I just stood there, gazing out over the endless array of reds, browns, and greys, changing color with the sunlight. The sun was setting on the desert and a great spiritual feeling came over me.

It was larger than life. My God, people were really nothing and all of us worrying about our petty little problems! It was magnificent.

We let Hedy run for a few more minutes and then I found another motel for the night. I was sure to make California the next day. I was so close.

During the last of the desert, Tim began to cry. It was time for him to eat so I stopped the car and filled the baby bottle again. I put the bottle in his mouth and he still cried. I tried again and he pushed it away and made a terrible face. Then he screamed and I stopped the car and tasted the milk. The heat of the desert had soured it, and there wasn't a gas station or a cafe in sight. He kept on screaming and I was getting very frightened. Sensing trouble, Chris and Mary began to cry.

There was nothing for me to do but drive on and on until I saw a place to get help. It seemed like miles but I finally spotted a cafe.

I stopped the car, grabbed a can of milk and a baby bottle and ran into the kitchen of the cafe.

"I've got to fix my baby a bottle—I'm sorry."

The cook was stunned. "Okay. All right," she said.

"Got any boiled water I can mix with this milk?"

"Won't take but a minute," the woman said, wiping her hands on her apron. She put a pan of water on to boil.

"The baby's formula went sour. Just a minute, I've got to go out and check on the kids," I frantically said.

I ran back to the car and Tim was still crying. Chris had lifted him into the back seat and was rocking him.

"It's almost ready, Chris. I'll be right back."

"Okay, Mommy."

I ran back in, poured the water and milk in the baby bottle, thanked the woman, and ran out. I put Tim back in the bassinet with the nipple in his mouth. He was quiet. I breathed deep and started the car again. When Tim finished the milk he fell sound asleep. For the rest of the trip I would have to fill the thermos with boiling water and mix each bottle separately.

I was so weary of traveling and that night I bought a pint instead of a half-pint. I drank about three-quarters of it and passed out.

Traveling was no longer pleasant because the weather was hot. I was on Route 66 going into Needles, California.

When we crossed the border into California we all got out of the car and kissed the ground.

I felt excited.

This it was going to be different. When Karl came home we were going to have a new and better life.

13

Housing was just as hard to find in Anaheim as it had been back east. I couldn't find Karl's friend and had to wire Doctor John for money.

The first night we stayed in a motel and the next day, after hours of looking, I found a furnished apartment. I paid the rent, bought a second-hand crib for Tim, and had twenty dollars left. I got a few groceries and a fifth of liquor. I sent my change of address to the Navy and hoped to God my next allotment check would reach me at my new address.

I had made it across the country and I was finally in California with no friends, two children, a baby, a dog, and seven pups. At that moment, all that really mattered was the liquor. It eased the pain of being in a strange land alone.

It didn't take long for me to figure out what was going on in the apartment house. Most of the tenants were young couples with small children and it was one constant party. Everyone knew everyone else and thought nothing of running in and out of each other's apartments. Pat and Lance who lived next door seemed to have the most money and the most parties. It was easy for me to party at their place and check on my babies at the same time. The people who came in and out were strangers but they pretended to be my closest friends.

There was quite a bit of swapping, with couples going off together into a bedroom or outside. That didn't interest me. I only wanted to stay full of alcohol, and at Pat's I could get all I wanted for free.

In the daytime, it was more and more difficult for me to take care of the simple household chores and the children. I had given all the puppies away. Chris was taking the bus to kindergarten, Mary was playing outside near an orange grove with the other children from the building, and Tim stayed in his crib.

Alcoholism had hit me hard. I managed to keep enough liquor to sip on in the daytime because my hangovers were unbearable. When I ran out of money, I borrowed from Pat and Lance, who didn't seem to mind at all.

Karl wrote that he would be home in five months and I took pictures of the children to send to him. One of the neighbors took a picture of me. I'm sure the dark circles under my eyes and my unkempt appearance were very revealing, but Karl's letters never mentioned them.

Soon I knew in my heart that I could not live without alcohol and money left my hands as fast as I got it. By the end of each month I was charging liquor at the corner liquor store and borrowing groceries from the neighbors. My allotment had come to my new address and all I did was pay the rent so we'd have some place to live. After that, I didn't care.

I was so weak and shaky that I couldn't even change Tim's diaper, and I never took him out of the crib for fear of dropping him. He lay on wet sheets in a wet diaper for days and all I gave him to eat was milk in a baby bottle that I never washed out. I just stayed drunk and Tim stood up in the crib and cried.

"Timmy, stop it!" Oh, God, I was so sick. Why didn't Karl come home? I couldn't stand it much longer. I was so sick. I couldn't do it. I couldn't take care of all these things. Oh, God, what was the matter with me? Why couldn't I pull myself together?

Eventually my neighbors knew I was an alcoholic and they didn't want anything to do with me. They stopped talking to me and inviting me to their parties and I knew why.

One afternoon when Chris came home from kindergarten I asked him to stay with the kids. I got in the car, drove to the liquor store, shuffled up to the counter, and said, "I'd like a fifth of vodka, please, and put it on my bill."

"I'm sorry, ma'am, we can't put anything more on your bill. You owe us sixty-five dollars now."

"I get my allotment in a few days and I'll pay my bill."

"No, ma'am. I talked it over with my partner and we decided not to give you any more credit."

I was not only sick, I was furious. "After all the money I spend in here?"

"Sorry, ma'am."

Then I was desperate. "Just one more? I'll pay my bill in a couple of days."

"I'm real sorry, ma'am."

Then I changed my tactics. "I'm having some friends in—ah—I'd really like to have it for this party."

The man turned his back on me and I pounded my fist on the counter. "Please! Please! Just this once! Please, can't you see I need it? Just this once, please!"

"Look, I'm in the liquor business and I don't mind selling it to you if you have the cash but I'm not going to help you kill yourself by giving you more credit. Look, why don't you forget it for today? Ma'am, I hate to say this, but you're sick."

I slowly turned around, grabbed my belly, and walked out.

Back at the apartment I looked around at the mess I'd made, turned the television on, couldn't sit still, paced, shook, and cried.

God, why didn't somebody help me? Oh, God, I needed a drink. I couldn't stand it. It wasn't fair. If only Karl would come home. Help me, help me. Why didn't Karl help me? Goddamn neighbors! I didn't give a damn if they didn't want to talk to me. I didn't have any money, any food. Messed up the whole thing again!

I tried again to sit in a chair and keep my nerves quiet. It didn't work.

Jesus, I had to have a drink. I couldn't go on. I couldn't even look at Timmy. I wished I were dead. If I killed us all we'd all be out of our misery! Yes, that's what I'd do. As soon as we were all together I'd turn on the gas and nobody would know the difference. The kids would just go to sleep and so would I.

I had made the decision because there just didn't seem to be anything else to do. Guilt kills and I had all the guilt in the world.

While I was planning all this in my mind there was a knock on the door. I didn't answer it and Pat and Lance walked right in.

"I've made a big pot of spaghetti. Okay if I take your kids and give them some?" Pat asked.

"I guess so," I whimpered.

"I had this extra quart of milk, too," Pat said, putting it in my refrigerator.

"Thank you." I tried to control my shaking and burst into tears. "I don't know what's wrong with me. I must have a cold or the flu or something."

"You talk to Lance and I'll bring you a plate, too."

"No, thank you. I couldn't eat—really."

Pat left with Chris and Mary.

Lance started right in. "You're having quite a problem, aren't you, Nancy?"

"Well, you see, it's that Karl hasn't been able to send me any extra money and I'm broke."

67

"Don't worry. We understand. We're going to loan you some groceries."

I died inside. I wanted money so I could get some relief for myself—a bottle.

"That won't be necessary. Just a couple of dollars would tide me over."

"I'm afraid we don't have a couple of dollars to loan you but we do have lots of food. You know, Nancy, you shouldn't stay cooped up in this apartment all the time. Isn't there something you'd like to do?"

"No. I have to take care of the children."

"You could take the children to the park. Maybe the amusement park, where they could ride on things."

"Maybe when Karl comes home."

"Isn't there something you did before you had children? I mean when you were younger?"

I closed my eyes. I didn't want to think. Why didn't he just give me some money?

"How about Pat and I watching the kids while you go swimming some day? Get away from the kids."

"No. We'll do things when Karl comes home."

"Can you swim?"

"A little. I used to ice-skate."

I sat up quickly. The words had slipped out. I hadn't thought about ice skating in years.

"You did? Hey, that's great."

He hit a soft spot. I fumbled around in my purse and pulled out the torn brown newspaper clipping. Lance was surprised and excited. He said he knew there was something I had done. I assured him it was a long time ago and all over.

"Say, I have an idea. There's a rink in Los Angeles. Let's get a baby sitter and go."

"Oh no. I couldn't go any place with my cold."

"I'll bet it would make you feel better."

"Don't be silly, Lance. I can't do that."

Lance got angry. "All right. What are you going to do—sit here and drink yourself to death? Anything's worth a try."

They had found me out. They knew and I knew that I would surely die without a drink. Pat returned, took charge of the children, arranged for a baby sitter, and helped me put on an old pair of torn slacks. I was getting sicker and sicker.

68

I was scared to go to the store—how was I going to go to Los Angeles?

In the car they tried to reassure me. But without any alcohol in my system I shook more and more.

We arrived at the rink. With great effort, I laced up the rented skates. Pat and Lance, already on the ice, had left me alone on purpose.

Slowly I moved onto the ice, holding onto the railing. It was several minutes before I worked up enough nerve to step out. I eased one skate in front of the other but there was no strength left in my legs to hold me up. Out in the middle, my legs collapsed, and I fell. I put my head down on the ice and cried. Pat and Lance came over to help.

"Leave me alone. I'm a clown. Can't you see? I'm a clown!"

No one said a word all the way home.

When I got out of the car I told them I was sorry and they said we would try it again sometime when I was stronger.

I couldn't imagine ever being strong again. My legs, once the most important thing to me, were shot. Everything that meant anything to me was gone, forever.

That night, my mind roared. I shook and tossed, and took eight aspirins to try to quiet the storm that was raging in my brain. Eventually I fell asleep.

The next day I had a letter from Karl saying that he was on his way home. I looked around at the messy apartment and knew I had to pull things together. I didn't want Karl to find out about my drinking and the fear that Lance would tell occupied my every thought. I had to cover up.

My allotment check arrived. I paid the liquor bill and the neighbors, and bought groceries. There was no liquor in the house when Karl got there. In fact, everything looked quite normal.

I threw my arms around Karl and kissed him. "I missed you so much," I said.

"I missed you too."

He looked at Tim crawling around on the floor all dressed and clean. "Wow, he's really grown."

I was so nervous I was even afraid Tim might speak and say, "This is the first time my mommy's taken me out of the crib."

Karl and the children talked and played while I tried desperately to fix something to eat.

Karl looked at me. "You got a drink?"

"No, I don't, but I can go to the liquor store and get something."

"Fine. We'll celebrate. We're leaving for San Diego tomorrow."

"Oh, Karl, that's great."

I knew if we could just get out of Anaheim no one would be able to tell Karl about me.

On our way to the liquor store, I felt everything was going to be all right again. A new house, a new town, and new friends. Then drinking wouldn't be a problem. After all, I had been very lonely.

We drove down Highway 101 into San Diego. San Diego, nestled along the shores of the blue Pacific Ocean, was the prettiest sight I'd ever seen.

14

Housing was more of a problem than ever. The only place we could find was temporary Navy housing— a quonset hut. We drove down the street past rows and rows of quonsets and finally reached the rental office.

The whole project was surrounded by dirt and I had to squint my eyes to keep out the flying dust. We were assigned a quonset hut. Everything in the hut was identical to the Federal housing in Texas. The wooden arms on the couch, the worn leather cushions, the cracked dishes, and the pans thick with black. Even the cockroaches.

After we settled in I made up my mind to control my drinking. I wanted to start fresh. It soon was clear that it didn't matter—everyone was drinking. The fact that the men had been in Korea and were reunited with their families was reason enough for one continuing party.

Not one day went by that a case of beer wasn't brought into the quonset. Many times Karl just brought it and other times I asked for it.

Most of the families were living the same way. Men stayed out late at the club, came home drunk, fought with their wives, and everyone stayed in that state. I never could figure out why the men had all the fun.

Although Karl drank heavily, he didn't overlook the fact that I was drinking as much as he was.

"We can't afford all this beer," Karl said.

"I wish you'd stay home once in a while. Do you have to go out every night?"

"I don't go out every night. I have a couple of beers at the club. So what? You get your share."

"Can't we just talk?"

"What d'you want me to say?"

"I'm sure we could think of something but all you do when you're home is fall asleep."

"I'm tired. I do have to work, you know. We're trying to get the ship ready to go back to Korea."

I opened another beer.

I don't remember how long Karl was home—just long enough for me to get pregnant again. Because I was drunk most of the time I not only didn't care about sex with Karl but didn't bother with birth control either. I got out of having sex as much as I could and when we did do it I prayed that he would hurry up and get it over. I can't really explain my feelings except I had an aching inside me that I didn't understand. Karl was interested in everything else but me and when he was through drinking with his buddies and being important in his Navy career, then it was my turn.

I was never excited by other men that I saw and met, either. I had given in to the idea that this was the way it was supposed to be. At times I wondered if there were any married people that were happy.

My correspondence with Grandma and Mother was sparse. I didn't want to tell them the truth about me or about our marriage. I felt that things would get better and then I could write to them. I knew things would be better—some day.

When Karl left again, I didn't care about anything, not even the people that lived around me. Staying in the quonset hut until Karl returned just depressed me but in another sense I was relieved. I could be myself and drink all I wanted to without his criticism. The same old routine started again only this time I drank only wine. I couldn't afford liquor. I staggered around the hut trying to take care of the children and eventually got so bad that I passed out in the daytime.

A few months later a neighbor rushed into my hut. "Your husband's ship hit a mine! I saw it on the news!"

"Oh, my God!" I screamed.

I quickly turned on the television—nothing. I ran to the corner phone booth and called the newspaper. The man read the list of dead. Karl was not on it.

The next few days I sat in front of the television with my bottle of wine and watched the news. The destroyer had hit a mine, had sailed backwards into Kuri, Japan, and would be limping home with a temporary bow.

Karl arrived home in January and had orders to Astoria, Oregon. Chris and Mary would have to change schools again and the new baby was due in March.

We packed everything again and drove to Astoria. There was a nice duplex waiting for us and a Navy hospital. My doctor believed in "childbirth without fear" and talked to me at great length about how it would work. It was a new idea at that time. He explained to me about breathing properly and that the only thing he would use would be a shot of novocaine. In the delivery room I was fully awake when the baby started to be born. The doctor sounded worried and I asked him to tell me what was wrong. It seems that the afterbirth was coming before the baby's head and he was trying to push the afterbirth back up inside me. I panicked. He quickly shoved a long something up inside of me which I later found out was the novocaine. The pain stopped and somehow David was born.

There was also a problem of Rh negative and when I was back in my hospital bed the doctor came to me and said my baby might have to have a complete transfusion. They gave him Vitamin K and never had to give the transfusion. I went home first and left David in the hospital until they were sure he would be all right. Then I was finally able to bring him home. Every morning after Karl left for his ship, my baby would spend about five minutes shaking. I told Karl and he said I was imagining it. One day David was having a convulsion just as Karl walked in the door. When he saw that I hadn't been lying we took David back to the hospital. He remained there for four more weeks and after that seemed healthy.

As for me, I was always trying to heal up from having a baby and it was getting rather tiresome. I decided to try the rhythm method of birth control.

We had been in Oregon just a little while when Karl got orders to Guam. I couldn't stay in that housing because if your husband was transferred you had to leave too. Karl said he would have to go first and then he would send for us.

"I might as well take you back to San Diego. I know you can stay in a quonset hut until I can send for you."

"Oh, Karl."

"What the hell do you want me to do? I'm in the Navy and the Navy comes first. I can't help that."

"But the quonsets? Those cockroach-ridden, bug-infested messes?"

"So you think you've got it bad. Well, let me tell you something about my mother. She and my dad came over here from Germany and he was mean. I mean, really mean to my mother. They lived on a farm and there were nine of us to take care of. She didn't have a washer or a laundromat. In fact, she had to carry water from a stream and wash our clothes behind my dad's back. He didn't want her to take the time from working in the fields to even wash our clothes. She's cooked on a wood stove all her life and to this day has never complained about anything. She didn't guzzle booze like you do, either."

"All right, Karl. We'll live in San Diego. But, Karl, I'm *not* your mother!"

Each trip was getting more and more difficult for me. My nerves were getting worse and three kids fighting in the back seat while I held the new baby didn't help.

We arrived in San Diego and found everything the same—even the cockroaches!

15

Once again I felt relieved when Karl left for Guam. My boss was gone and I could do anything I wanted to. I remember we had hauled an old television set around with us and it never worked right in a quonset hut. I took all the children, drove to a television shop, and bought twenty-five feet of antenna wire. I hooked it up to the back of the television set and threw the long piece of wire all over the floor of the quonset until the picture came in perfectly. I was very pleased with myself that I had solved the problem. Also I was getting a very big kick out of my favorite program, "Topper." I loved Neil, the martini-drinking St. Bernard.

We had left Hedy in Oregon with some people who really loved her because it was against the housing rules to have a dog in a quonset hut. They had given us special permission the first time, but that was it.

Neil was planting ideas in my drunken head.

All children should have a dog. What a stupid rule to have. You'd have thought they were renting mansions or something. Well, I'd get a Neil for the children. It was only fair. A Neil would be a wonderful pet.

I was getting very drunk and I sent Chris to the store to buy a paper. I looked through all the ads and found a St. Bernard for sale. I had just received my allotment check and had a little money. The last thing I remember was seeing "St. Bernard For Sale."

The next morning, when I woke up, I was really hungover. My whole body shook and I had to have a drink. I struggled to get up, walked to the tiny kitchen, and saw it. Tied to the cupboard door was a full-grown black and tan Doberman pinscher.

Oh, my God! Jesus, it was going to attack me.

The dog did nothing but look at me. I saw some papers on the kitchen table and picked them up. There was a receipt for fifty dollars and pedigree papers. Her name was Lady.

I woke Chris and asked him how we got the dog. He said we drove to some people's house and bought it.

"All of us?"

"Oh yeah, Mom. We took David and everybody."

I didn't remember a thing and it really frightened me.

I walked to the dog and said, "Nice girl, nice girl." She seemed happy and not vicious at all. I poured myself a drink of wine and settled my nerves. Then I untied

Lady and let her run through the quonset hut. She licked all the children and when I told her to sit—she sat. The papers showed that she was eight months old. She came with a choke-chain and a heavy leash and after I fed and dressed the children I took her for a short walk.

She was magnificent and I felt a surge of power just having her near me. I knew that we were going to be friends. Maybe she would have the power that I didn't have.

It wasn't long before she was a part of our family and the talk of the quonset-hut community.

I let her loose in the mornings to run all over the area and get exercise. She always came back when I called her. Of course it wasn't long before the management knew about her.

After I had taken care of the children I sat on the wooden front stoop and watched Lady run. Or I would run up and down the rows of huts with her. I always had my glass of wine handy, though. I never got too far away from it.

I saw the housing manager coming down the small sidewalk. He stopped when he saw me and yelled, "You have to get rid of that dog."

"I'm not going to."

"It's against the rules and regulations."

"So what?"

"I'll have to take steps."

"Take one more step and I'll sick her on you!"

The manager turned around and ran away from our row of quonsets.

Several times he tried the same thing and each time I warned him to stay away from me, my family, and my dog. I guess he got tired of trying because he finally left us alone.

It wouldn't be the last time I used Lady.

16

Lady was never mean. In fact she was friendly with everyone and everyone loved her. The children lay on her to watch television and she followed them around when they were outside playing. She took better care of them than I did. I was drinking more and more and telling myself that I was not an alcoholic, that I was stuck with great responsibilities and deserved to have something for myself.

For Christmas of 1952 I managed to buy a few toys and another Navy wife and I shared Christmas dinner. Her husband was gone, too. After dinner the children went outside to play with their toys and she and I decided to go out. We had done our Santa Claus duty and needed a reward. She arranged for baby sitters and we went to a bar.

Most of my drinking, up until then, had been at home and when I slid onto the red bar-stool I wondered why I hadn't thought about going out before. People were drinking and laughing and I felt warm and good inside, like being in the womb or going to church. After several drinks and with what I'd had in the daytime, I was getting very drunk. A sailor sat beside me and started talking to me. I must have gone into a blackout again because all I remember is leaving the bar with him.

When I woke, the following morning, I couldn't remember how I'd gotten into bed, or for that matter, how I'd gotten home. I jumped up to see if the children were okay and semen ran down my leg. I checked the children and then sat on the edge of my bed trying to remember what had happened.

Oh my God, what had I done?

I rushed to the cupboard and poured myself a straight shot of gin. The last of the Christmas cheer. It wasn't going to be enough so I washed my face and my crotch and went to the store for a bottle of wine.

Two months later I knew I was pregnant and my world collapsed. This was one I couldn't get out of and Karl would kill me. I fell into a state of complete and utter despair. I cried and drank more. The only person I felt I could confide in was the Navy wife, Francie.

"If I don't get something done, I'll kill myself."

"Don't do anything yet. I can get some pills for you. Damn men anyway. They just screw and disappear."

I took all the pills Francie could get me but I did not abort.

Letters were coming from Karl telling me to get overseas shots for myself and the children. We were on a housing list and our name would be coming up soon. He was glad I wasn't pregnant because a pregnant wife couldn't travel to Guam.

My next allotment came and I drank more and more. I had switched to gin and all I wanted to do was blank everything out of my mind. Francie kept bringing me pills. I took them all, not even knowing what they were. They made me sleep and they were red. It wasn't long before I was asking Francie to bring me more and more pills. I hated what I was doing and I hated my own body. I didn't want to be a carrier of babies, especially a baby whose father I didn't even remember, let alone know.

The pills made my craving for alcohol stronger and the alcohol forced me to take the pills when I couldn't sleep. Francie was certain if I'd just take the pills I'd be all right. Alcohol was my original habit and I stuck with it. But the pills had become a habit too. Later in life I realized that an addict is an addict no matter what the drug is.

Francie soon grew disgusted with me and stopped providing my pills. That meant I had to drink more and it also meant I was alone—again. Everything was getting hazier and hazier and the days were all melting into one. I tried to keep the children fed and that was the extent of my effort. I am certain they lived mostly on peanut butter and hot dogs. I hadn't spanked my children very hard but now I was beating them. They couldn't open their mouths to laugh or make any noise that I didn't go into a rage. That increased my guilt and made me hate myself even more.

What was wrong with me? Why didn't someone help me before I killed my children? Oh God, please!

The children were frightened and stayed in their bedrooms when I was raving. The more they stayed out of my way the less chance I had of taking my hate for living out on them.

One night I was sitting in a chair thinking my brain was popping right out of my head. I was desperate.

If I was dead it would all be over. There's no use in living, really, I thought.

I walked to the kitchen and got a knife out of the drawer and slowly walked back and sat down with it. I had put it to my wrists and closed my eyes when a new thought overtook me. I threw the knife down, ran out the door to the phone booth, and called the Navy chaplain. "Come quick—come help me—quick—hurry—I need help now!"

In fifteen minutes he was in my hut. In that fifteen minutes I had pulled all the empty bottles out of the cupboards and stacked them on the floor.

"See, see what's happening? Now help me! Do something to help me! I can't stand it another minute!"

I waited. I looked at the Navy chaplain in his blue uniform with all the gold on it. The picture of authority and a man who could certainly do something with all his power. He stood in the middle of the floor.

"Let us pray," he said.

"Oh, Lord, our heavenly Father, watch over this family. Let them be peaceful and happy. Let them gather into the fold and see the light. Amen."

"Is that all?"

"Yes, my dear, that's all."

"Oh, Jesus Christ! I'm sure glad I didn't ask you a big one like, 'who's God?' " I screamed.

The hand at the end of the three gold stripes took my hand and told me everything would be all right. He left.

I flung myself down on the bed.

Why hadn't he done something? What was wrong with me? Oh God, the pain. I couldn't stand the pain in my stomach.

I went to the kitchen, poured another drink, and it wouldn't go down. After vomiting, I tried another and it stayed down but the pain didn't go away. I couldn't get relief even with alcohol which usually numbed all pain.

I wanted a pill.

It occurred to me that a hospital corpsman lived across from me and I walked right over to his hut and asked him for some sleeping pills. He gave them to me but made me promise to go to the hospital the next day. I promised.

The next day I felt better. I got up, fed the children their cereal, played with them a little, and started to do a load of washing.

It must have been something I ate. I was okay again. I

was certainly not an alcoholic. I was just lonesome and how was I going to tell Karl I couldn't go to Guam because I was pregnant?

Nipping the gin, I was able to finish washing the clothes. About four in the afternoon the pain hit again. I thought I was having a miscarriage and prayed I was. This time the pain was so excruciating and I screamed so hard that the neighbors came running. They called the Navy hospital, the ambulance came, and the corpsmen put me on a stretcher. The children were playing outside and David was in his crib. The neighbors kept telling me not to worry—that they would take care of my children and my dog.

Chris, who was eight then, stood outside the quonset hut.

"Mommy, Mommy, where are you going?' he cried.

I couldn't answer him. I just glanced at his young wrinkled forehead as they wheeled me by him.

In the hospital I told the nurse that I was having a miscarriage. The doctor came in and examined me and the nurse with the two gold stripes said, "You are not having a miscarriage."

"Then what's wrong with me? I've got a terrible pain."

The nurse pulled her shoulders back. "If you don't know what's wrong with you by now, you never will."

"Can I have a sleeping pill?"

"No, dear, you aren't getting any medication."

"But I can't sleep."

"I'm sorry, but those are orders."

I watched the stiff-starched uniform go out the door.

I couldn't sleep and withdrawal was getting more painful all the time. I had reached a point where the fear of stopping my addiction was more than I could bear. I was in a situation in that hospital where I had to withdraw and there was nothing I could do about it. Oh, how I needed a pill or a drink! I hurt, I sweated, I shook, and I wanted to die. By morning I had completed my trip into reality, and the mess I'd made of my life loomed before me like a giant villain.

What had I done? My poor children. Karl. Oh God, I couldn't think about it. Why couldn't I stop drinking? I was not stupid. And why was everyone so merciless?

On the third day I saw the chaplain standing in the doorway.

82

"How are you, my dear?"

I remembered being cross with him when he came to see me. "I'm fine. When can I go home to my children?"

He sat down in a chair by my bed and I noticed he looked a lot like Doctor John.

"You stay here and get well. Your children are being well cared for," he said.

"Where are they?"

"They're fine. Now don't worry."

"I want my husband home to help me. I can't go to Guam like he wants me to."

"I'm trying to get him home on humanitarian shore duty."

"Oh, that's nice of you. I still want to know where my children are. The neighbors said they would watch them."

"The neighbors couldn't take care of them so the Welfare Department put them in a foster home."

"The Welfare Department!" I screamed.

"They're getting good care and the neighbors just couldn't take care of them all."

I put my head in the pillow and sobbed.

Two days later the chaplain informed me that Karl was on his way home from Guam and would be flying in the next day. I wasn't allowed to have my children back until he arrived. I could leave the hospital, however, so the chaplain drove me home to my quonset hut. He left and I walked in and saw the mess. The washer was full of dirty clothes and smelling.

My neighbor came over with Lady. "We kept the dog for you."

He left and I was stunned.

They couldn't keep the children but they took my dog? What were people doing? What right did anyone have to take my children away from me? All I did was drink a little. So I got a little sick from it—that doesn't make me an alcoholic.

Then it dawned on me that Karl was coming home.

Oh God, I had to clean up the mess. What was he going to do to me? He'd kill me. I'd explain. The best thing I could do was not drink, and clean up the mess.

I fed Lady and started cleaning but I was aware of being sober, alone, scared, and weak.

That night, after scrubbing and cleaning, I took a

shower and went to bed early. With no liquor or pills I couldn't sleep. It was quiet without the children but noises did come from other quonsets—parties and people laughing. It seemed forever but I finally dozed off.

The next morning Karl came down the narrow walk carrying his suitcase. He looked tall, straight, and masculine in his khaki uniform, as though he could conquer anything—win wars, fight battles, and move mountains.

I ran to him and clung. He didn't respond and I knew that the chaplain had told him I was pregnant. We walked into the hut.

"It's time to go pick up the children," he said in his most stern voice.

"I'm ready."

We drove twenty miles out into the country where the children were being kept. I tried to talk to Karl. "I'm sorry."

"You're always sorry. I don't want to talk about it."

At that moment I hated Karl. I felt like I was beating my head against a stone wall. I wondered if he was human.

I fantasized being at the Olympics. The flame was trying to touch the sky. My clothes were perfect and the gun went off. I skated like a flash of lightning and won. The crowd yelled and I walked up to accept my gold medal.

Karl went into the foster home first and then called to me. My children ran to me and cried. David was standing up in a crib in the bedroom. I picked him up and hugged him.

Chris was really happy to see me. "Mom, I ate twenty pancakes for breakfast."

"Wow, that's a lot," I answered, trying not to cry.

That evening I fixed a meatloaf and after supper bathed the children and put them to bed. Karl had gone out and come back with a fifth of liquor. When I sat down to rest, he opened the liquor and poured himself a large drink.

"Where's mine?" I asked.

"You, my dear, don't get any."

I thought I was going to have a nervous breakdown watching Karl drink.

"One won't hurt me. Please?"

"I said no!"

"Why do you have to drink in front of me, then?"

"Look—let's get one thing straight. From now on and for the rest of my life I'm going to take any woman I can get and drink what I want to when I want to. Do you hear that?"

I watched Karl drink four more drinks and leave.

I yelled, "Where are you going?"

"Out. I'm going to take a walk."

As soon as he was out of sight I ran for the bottle and got a drink. Relief at last. I waited a minute and then took another drink. A sweeping euphoric feeling engulfed me.

Let him come back. I didn't give a damn.

When Karl returned I was relaxed, watching television. The commercial was blaring the attributes of Lucky Lager beer. Karl rushed at me and pulled me up out of the chair.

"You slut! Who in the hell do you think you are? And pregnant with someone else's kid!"

"Karl, stop. Wait. I can explain."

"Shut up! You're not going to explain anything to me."

"Please, Karl, you're hurting me."

He slapped my face several times.

"You got into the booze, didn't you?"

"Karl, stop. You're drinking, too."

"That's my business, pig. I told you you're not going to drink."

He pushed me down into the corner of the hut, doubled his fists and beat me in the face. It felt like ten thousand bombs were hitting me and I was completely helpless to stop them.

I screamed and the children got out of bed. David began crying from his crib and Karl kept on beating me.

"Get back in bed," he bellowed at the children.

They huddled together and went back to bed.

He stopped beating my face, but then he took hold of my long hair and swung my head against the wall, again and again. As he stepped back, large hunks of hair lay in his hand.

My face was bleeding, my eyes were swollen, and I slumped. Karl stormed out.

Chris, Mary, and Tim came out of their bedroom and helped me to a chair. They stood by for an explanation.

"Mom, why do you stay with Dad?" Chris asked.

I put my arms around my children. "Everything's all right now, kids. Don't worry, I'm going to be all right."

"But Daddy hurt you. You're crying," Mary said. Her big brown eyes were searching for an answer.

"Come on, let's go back to bed now."

"Mommy, your face is bleeding," Mary cried. "I'll get you a washcloth."

"No. I'll take care of it. You kids go back to bed."

"Where's Lady? We want Lady," Chris said.

"Your father let her out. I'll get her for you."

They all dutifully went to bed. I went to the front door and called Lady in. Even though Karl was a part of the family he wouldn't have dared hit me in front of her.

I washed my face, finished the bottle, and went to bed. Just before I dozed off I thought about how frightened my children were and how I was incapable of doing anything about it.

17

Karl acted as if nothing had happened, and he drove the children and me to look at some tract homes that were for rent. I didn't much care. I felt terrible and was ashamed of my black-and-blue face. And now I was desperately afraid of Karl.

We moved out of the quonset hut into a three-bedroom home. Our Sears furniture had been in storage since Newport and I was happy to see it again. A new lawn was coming up and I planted flowers around the front and side of the new house.

Although Karl was silent most of the time and I constantly wondered what he was thinking, I felt a tiny bit of dignity coming back. Part of it was because I took pride in my new home.

It wasn't long before we both started drinking but we agreed that neither one of us would drink too much. The house was costing more than we had been paying so we decided to make home-brew.

Being so afraid of Karl, I drank when he wasn't home. I bought wine and hid it under the mattress. Then when he came home we drank home-brew together. Of course Karl was stopping off at the bars with his buddies so we were both getting our share.

Susan was born September 25, 1953. Emotionally, I was confused. I loved my new baby but didn't know what Karl was going to do or how he would act. I was always waiting for the bomb to fall for all the sins I had committed and when he came to the hospital to pick up Susan and me I put the baby blanket over her face so Karl wouldn't have to look at her. Karl and I didn't speak and when we got home I quickly put Susan in the back bedroom in her bassinet. From then on I only tended to her when necessary and whatever love she got was from the other children. They thought she was great.

One day Mother telephoned. She told me that Doctor John was dead. I was shocked. She said he had gotten very senile—shooting at imaginary people out his bedroom window, putting on two pairs of socks, and continually thinking that someone was stealing his Packard or his money.

"I guess he had you on his mind because he was saying funny thing like, 'I've arranged for you to go to secretarial school, Nancy,' " Mother said.

"What else?"

"Grandma isn't too well, either. She had to put Doctor John in the hospital. She acted very strange about it. Almost glad."

"What's going to happen to her?"

"If she keeps acting funny, Howard and I will have to take her back to the hospital. We've been thinking about moving in with her but she says she doesn't want anybody."

"Oh, Mother, don't take her back there."

"You never understood, Nancy. She loves it there. She has all kinds of women friends and can talk and act exactly as she wants, too. How are all your children?"

"They're fine. It's a hard job though."

"Well, Nance, don't give up your whole life for your children. Why don't you go to work for a while?"

"Mother! How can I go to work?"

"Find someone to watch the children and go. Work is good for your soul."

I felt very mad at Mother.

What was I supposed to do? Leave them like she did us? Never!

I realize now that it was just an excuse because I was being protected and I was free to drink.

Doctor John dead? Doctor John senile? That drunk Howard was going to try and put Grandma away and get Doctor John's money. Come to think of it, I could use a little of that money myself. If we just had more money our life would straighten out, I knew.

I took another swig of wine.

Orders came for Karl again. He was being transferred to San Francisco. I didn't want to leave the only house we'd ever had so we agreed that he would come home on weekends. He was to send me money from his paycheck to supplement my allotment. I was going to be paying all the bills. Nothing came and Karl didn't come home for what seemed like weeks. I wrote and wrote for extra money, but nothing came.

I needed more money to pay bills and support my habit. Ideas started forming in my mind.

Maybe I could go to work? What would I do with the children? At least I wouldn't have to depend on Karl. He was angry about Susan anyway.

I was talking to my neighbor over the fence one day,

telling her I'd like to go to work. She gave me a phone number to call that would give me information on how to get a woman to work for me. I thought it over and decided I'd better get a job first. I dressed in the best I had. Chris watched the children and I went to the largest department store in San Diego to apply. I got a job as a salesclerk, in the sportswear department. My starting salary was $1.25 an hour.

I was so happy. I felt that maybe I was worthwhile after all. When I got home I called the number for the woman and a very secretive, low voice gave me an address to go to in the Mexican section of town. I pulled up in front of an old shacky-looking house, got out of the car, and went to the door. I looked inside and saw pews as though it was a church. A Mexican man, dressed like a minister, motioned to me to come in. I explained why I was there and he again, without speaking, motioned to me to follow him. I followed him out a back door, down a trash-littered alley, and through another door into a small, dark room with one lightbulb hanging from a cord. By now I was scared but at the same time excited, like I was really mixed up in a spy story of some kind.

I stood still in the dark room and waited. In a few minutes a Mexican man and a tiny Mexican woman came through another door. She and I stood there looking at each other. She smiled. Then the first words were spoken.

"This is Carmen," the man said.

"Hi," I said.

She smiled again.

The man said to Carmen, "You go with lady."

We gathered up Carmen's belongings, some loose and some in falling-apart cardboard boxes. Immediately I discovered that Carmen couldn't speak a word of English and I knew absolutely no Spanish. We drove home in silence.

The children were all waiting to see the new babysitter, I told her the children's names, and she pointed to all of them and said, "Chiquitas."

I asked, "Children?" and she nodded.

After I showed her her bedroom and everyone felt comfortable, I poured myself a glass of wine. I asked her if she wanted some by picking up the bottle and she said, "Sí." I found out later that she kept several bottles of

wine in her bedroom. In fact, Carmen and I were blood
sisters.

Carmen was an experience. She wore no bra and didn't
think it was necessary for little children to wear clothes.
When the clotheslines were full she laid the clothes on the
ground to dry. She took a bath every single day and carried the baby around on her hip all the time. If any baby
ever got love, Susan did.

Carmen brought me a cup of coffee every morning
while I was dressing for work. My new job made me very
nervous as I couldn't drink until lunch and then I was
afraid to have more than two for fear of acting drunk.
Immediately after work I stopped at a liquor store and
bought a fifth of wine. Then I pulled over to the side of
the road, leaned down below the seat and gulped. What
a relief! I was still making home-brew in a crock under
the sink and when I checked it at night I could tell it was
down about an inch. I told Carmen that green beer
would make her sick and then we laughed and sat at the
kitchen table with our wine. I had a blackboard I used
to write notes on and we taught each other a few words.
Even though we had a communication problem, we
understood—we were sisters. After a few weeks it was
more apparent.

I found a box of baby clothes in the garage and I asked
Carmen if they were hers. We were both drinking and
ended up crying on the floor of the hallway with the
baby clothes.

It took a long time and many drinks but I found out
all about Carmen.

She had five children in Mexico and her mother was
taking care of them. That is where she sent her fifteen
dollars every week. One child was crippled and they
never had enough to eat. She had, at one time, come to
the United States legally. She indicated by touching her
hair that the authorities had cut it short when they inspected her for diseases. Somewhere along the way she
lost her passport. Then she pulled out a picture of a
man—her husband. She put her hands in prayer position
and pointed upward to tell me he had died. She cried
and cried. She continued telling me about a big fat man
who told her he would take care of her in this country.
She lived with him, got pregnant, had the baby, and her
baby got pneumonia. The big fat man beat her and

90

wouldn't get a doctor for her baby. She put her hands in prayer position again to show that the baby had died. The baby clothes were her dead baby's.

I was bringing home $37.00 a week, paying Carmen $15.00, and buying groceries and wine with the rest. Karl came home a couple of weekends and made fun of Carmen and me. He told me that I'd never be able to hold a job because I was a drunk. There was something about Karl at the time, however, that made me think he was really hoping that I could work. Maybe he was hoping that working would solve my problem.

After two months of this hectic life and the neighbors complaining about Carmen I decided to quit. I fought with one neighbor.

"She lets those children run around naked."

"So what? She takes good care of them."

"And she flops around with no bra on."

"Maybe we ought to try that!" I said furiously.

"She has them doing exercises, naked, in front of your picture window—where everyone can see!"

It wasn't the nosy neighbors, it was the fact that the money just wasn't enough to keep things going so I had to tell Carmen I was not going to work and I'd have to let her go. She told me she would stay on without pay. We stayed home together for a week and then I packed her up in my car and took her back to the fake church where I had first seen that beautiful smile. We both hugged and cried and finally said goodbye.

I cried all the way home because I didn't know what was going to become of my sister Carmen.

A few weeks later the authorities came to my house and asked me questions about Carmen. I told them I didn't know anything about her.

18

I continued to make beer in the crock and when one batch was done, I'd bottle it, put it in the garage, and start another. I liked wine better but the beer was my security. If the money ran out I drank the beer.

The garage cupboards were full of beer and I kept right on making more.

One day Mary ran into the house. "Mommy, Mommy, there's a loud noise in the garage. Come quick and see."

I ran out to the garage and found all the beer blowing up, one right after the other.

"Oh, no! Mary, run into the house and get all the pans and pitchers you can find—hurry."

"What's wrong, Mommy?"

"It's blowing up, stupid! Can't you see? Now get me some pans!"

Mary came back with one pan.

"You brat! I said all you can! Never mind, I'll get them myself."

Beer and brown glass covered the garage floor and the beer was running underneath the big garage door, down the driveway, and out onto the street. Every second another bottle would pop.

I got all the containers I could, opened the bottles of green beer that hadn't popped, and poured it as fast as I could into the containers. As I poured, I drank, and after I cleaned up the mess, I spent the rest of the day drinking green beer.

* * *

In the spring of 1954 Karl received orders to Annapolis, Maryland. I was getting very weary of moving and traveling but each time I knew it would be the answer to my problem. A fresh start always sounded hopeful. In my gut I really wanted to be a good mother and I was certain I wasn't an alcoholic. It was all so confusing because I could never figure out why I couldn't stop drinking and I was stuck with so many guilts that they overwhelmed me. I couldn't stand thinking about my children, my life, or Karl. When I saw other wives functioning quite well, it just added to my guilts. I tried so damn hard to play the right role, and always failed.

We decided to drive across country. Now there were Chris, Mary, Tim, David, Susan, Karl, Lady, and me. The packing, yelling at kids, the dog running around worried, Karl and I arguing—moving was a chaotic mess.

I kept on drinking while the Navy movers were crating everything and I finally passed out on the floor. The next morning when it was time to leave I got the diapers, the formula, and the children into the car. My head throbbed. Karl got in the car and when we drove away I looked back at the only decent home I'd ever had since I had left Doctor John's. I swallowed hard.

After we were out of San Diego and on the highway Karl said, "There's a six-pack on the floor."

I looked at Karl and then at the beer. "Oh, Karl, you saved my life. Thanks."

I quickly opened a can, took a drink, and handed it to Karl. He took a drink and handed it back. The rest of the trip was a nightmare. The children crackling crackers, tugging and fighting for toys, tearing books. Susan crying. Pieces of bread and baloney all over the back seat. Karl refusing to buy any more alcohol to numb it all.

I tried to keep order and when I screamed Karl said, "Oh, shut up—kids are kids."

*　　*　　*

Maryland had seasons. I hadn't seen snow in a long time and it reminded me of happy winters on the ice. I couldn't think about it too much, though—it hurt.

Karl moved us into three different houses in Annapolis. The last one was twenty miles out in the country and I knew it was to keep me away from alcohol and stores where I could buy it. Nothing stopped me. Once more I got out the old crock and talked Karl into making beer. Many nights Karl didn't come home or came home late. I guess he had a hard time figuring how I could let such a beautiful house get so dirty. But it was so big and besides I really didn't care.

Karl had rented the house from a commander. Two stories, five bedrooms, five fireplaces, and long windows with green shutters. It looked as though Scarlett O'Hara, with her hoopskirts and picture hat, would step out on the long porch at any moment. Instead, I did. Feeling hump-shouldered, unkempt, and like a frightened animal. I was really very sick, and total isolation didn't help.

"Why don't you bring some friends home, Karl?"

"So you can get drunk and make a fool of me?"

"I won't get drunk, I promise."

"How are you going to manage that? Every time I come home you're drunk."

"You drink, Karl."

"I'm not the one with the problem. You are."

"I'm sick of you telling me that! Goddamn it, you've stuck me out here in the country where I don't even have a neighbor to talk to. What in the hell do you expect me to do?"

Karl wanted to go out and I kept screaming at him. When I saw that he was serious about leaving I changed my tactics. I walked over and put my arms around him. I really wanted him to stay because the old house scared me.

"Let's go to bed."

"How can I make love to you when you smell of stale beer all the time?"

That made me furious. "Come to think about it, I vaguely remember you making love to me when I had too much to drink. Is it more fun when I'm almost passed out? Sometimes when I wake up in the morning I know you've screwed me and I call that rape!"

"Shut up. You're insane. I ought to have you committed."

"Okay, Karl."

Moments passed and then Karl spoke softly. "I do know a couple I'd like to bring home to dinner. A guy I work with and his wife."

"When?"

"How about tomorrow night?"

"I'll fix spaghetti. Is that all right?"

"Fine with me."

"Can I have the car tomorrow to get groceries?"

"You'll have to take me all the way to work but I can ride back with them."

I rushed around getting the house cleaned, getting the groceries, and two half-gallons of wine.

I tried to dress up and found that I hadn't bought anything since Karl and I were married.

At three o'clock I started cooking the spaghetti and drinking the wine. By the time the company arrived, I was on my way. Karl was furious and did what he always did—stood in front of me and stared into my glassy eyes. He didn't speak but I knew that look. I clumsily got the spaghetti on the table, chatting wildly all the time.

"I'm so glad Karl brought some friends home. You see, he never brings anyone home. He'd rather hang over

94

a bar with his buddies. Can't blame him, though. You can see there's a million kids around here and the noise is enough to drive anyone crazy. I've asked him to take me to a bar but he says they're just for men. Now what's a woman to do, really?"

Karl calmly got up, walked over to me , and said, "Shut up. You're drunk."

When Karl sat down I carefully rose, picked up my plate of spaghetti and hit Karl directly over the head with it.   Karl got up and punched me right in the face as the couple ran out the door.

The children were crying and Karl was beating. I tried to get away and couldn't.

"Daddy, stop hitting our mother," Chris wailed.

Karl kept on beating and finally got me on the bed. "I'll show you, or else! You're going to stop this drinking!"

Karl punched and punched until I was out cold.

When I woke up I found myself in nothing but my bra. I got up and looked in the mirror and could hardly see out of either eye. My face looked exactly like it did the last time. Black-and-blue. Dried blood around my mouth.

Oh my God, what had I done? He knew me. Karl knew I was no damn good but I couldn't take another beating. Maybe if I stopped drinking he'd stop. Or maybe I should divorce him.

"I'm in a play at school. Daddy said he'd go and see me," Mary said.

"I'm glad Daddy can go. I'm not feeling well," I answered.

"It's okay, Mommy."

"But I should go. I really should."

Karl walked in from work. "Can't very well go looking like that."

"I'm sorry. Maybe I can go to the next one."

"It's always the next time. Come on, Mary, let's fix the kids something to eat so we can go."

"I'll fix it," I said.

"You better go to bed. We'll take care of ourselves. I'm taking the boys, too. You can manage Susan, can't you?"

Susan was asleep and I lay on the bed. The house was so big and quiet. I began to hear noises.

It must have been the furnace rattling. But what was that other noise?

I got up, looked in on Susan, and stood at the top of the long stairway, listening. I heard it again. My heart pounded. Carefully I walked downstairs and there it sat, all by itself, in the corner of the dining room—an ancient grand piano that the Commander had left in the house. He had told us that it was too valuable to ship. I stared at its claw-like carved legs. They moved. I jumped back and shook my head. The legs moved again. They were moving toward me. Then two large eyes popped open. Step by step the monster came toward me. I let out a loud scream and ran back upstairs, yelling, "Oh, help me! Somebody help me!" I was longing for a drink and wondering how I could get past the monster to the beer.

I was petrified. When I eased my way back downstairs I backed all the way into the kitchen, watching the piano all the time. I grabbed a glass out of the cupboard, took the lid off the beer crock, sat on the floor, and dipped in.

When Karl and the other children came home I was still sitting there.

"You look good," Karl said snidely.

I didn't answer and he went upstairs to put the kids to bed. I could hear them all laughing and tussling.

Hell, they didn't need me. They liked him. He played and laughed with them.

I dipped in for another glass of green beer.

When things got quiet Karl came downstairs and stood over me like a drill sergeant. "Get up and go to bed."

"I don't want to."

"Stay there then. I'm going out."

"So go."

He slammed the door and I stayed on the floor. In a few minutes Mary came downstairs and sat beside me.

"Mommy, do you like Daddy?"

"Oh, I don't know, Mary. Go back to bed."

"I'm afraid of him."

"He wouldn't hurt you for the world. You're his favorite girl."

"Mommy, Daddy scared me tonight."

"What do you mean? What are you talking about?"

"When we were playing upstairs, he put his hand on me."

"What? Where?"

"Right here." She put her hand between her legs.

I jumped up. "Are you sure?"

"I thought it was naughty. He scared me. I got away."

I was in such a stupor it was hard for me to think.

"Come on, honey, I'll take you back to bed."

"Okay, Mommy."

I sat on the edge of Mary's bed. "I'll take care of it. I'll see that it never happens again. Do you hear me? You must trust me."

"Yes, Mommy."

"I really don't think Daddy meant anything by it. Now close your eyes and I'll sit here until you go to sleep."

"I love you, Mommy."

"I love you, too, Mary, and someday I'm going to be better. You wait and see."

Mary closed her eyes.

What could I do? If I accused him he'd say I was insane. I couldn't involve Mary. I'd divorce him. I'd have to. But how could I take care of all these children? That bastard! What could I do? He'd say I was boozed up again, like he always did. That I was imagining things.

Mary was asleep.

19

Every morning I woke with the same panicky feeling. So many children to worry about. So much work to do. Food to fix. Clothes to wash. School buses to catch. Dog to feed. Mice to trap. Such a big house. Steps to take. Mountains to climb. Everything magnified and whirling. The house getting dirtier and dirtier until I just couldn't think at all. So I'd sit down and have a beer or wine, if there was any. When I drank enough I didn't have to think. Those were my days in Annapolis.

I knew if things changed I'd be all right. If Karl would only listen and understand. I really didn't have a problem with drinking. I could stop any time I wanted to, but I never did.

Karl received orders to go to school in Alameda, California. With the packing and the preparation for the trip back across the United States, and Karl not buying any alcohol I was forced into not drinking. The first day it was very hard but after we got on the road I felt a little better. Actually it was the first time in seven years that I had not had any alcohol in my system. Karl still complained. He always knew how to get to me by mentioning the ironing I never did.

"How many times have we carried that ironing back and forth across the country?"

"Don't worry about it."

"My mother ironed for nine of us and never let it go like you do."

"I told you before, I'm not your mother."

"But it's part of your job."

"What is my job, Karl?"

"You're a mother, aren't you?"

"Is that all I am? Aren't I anything else? A person, maybe? Or a human being?"

"I will say you've been better on this trip. Now if you just don't start drinking when we get to Alameda."

"Are you going to quit too?"

"I'll quit if you do."

"Okay."

I wouldn't quit. I'd just have to be careful until we got to California. He wouldn't stop anyway. I really thought I could quit if I wanted to but I didn't do anything else and it wasn't hurting anyone. A little drink now and then was good for people. In fact, everyone drank.

By the time we arrived in Alameda my stomach was

screeching for alcohol and walking back into an apartment in Federal housing didn't help.

"Karl, it's the same furniture! It's the same everything!"

"This is the only place the Navy could get us."

The children ran into their bedrooms, claiming their beds, and Karl got the crib out of the car.

"Susan can sleep in a bed now," I said.

"If you want her to, but I can still set up the crib."

"Not now—later."

"Later?"

"Yes, I'm pregnant."

"Oh God, just what we need. Don't you ever take precautions?"

"Don't you?"

"Me? Why should I? You're the one that has them."

I rubbed my belly. "Yes, and I don't know if I can go through it again."

"It's a little late for that, isn't it?"

"I guess so."

"Well, you can't blame me for the last one."

"Karl, please."

"Nancy, I don't know what's wrong with you. My mother never made a production out of childbirth. That's what women are put here for. The old Indian women had them right in the fields, got right up, and started plowing again."

"Maybe they had the right idea but I'm not an old Indian woman, Karl."

"No, you're just a damn drunk."

"Karl, I'm trying, but how can I keep on when you say things like that to me."

"You've tried before and it never worked. Look, this school means a lot to me and I'm going to have to study hard. I can't be worrying about you all the time so will you please stay sober? My whole Navy career is at stake."

Every night Karl studied in the bedroom and I watched television. I didn't drink. I tried to encourage him and told him everything would be fine. He was so impressed that one night he bought a six-pack of beer. My stomach stopped hurting and the world looked rosy again.

99   Like a thief in the night, King Alcohol grabbed my

soul again. One beer and it was too late. So when Karl left for school the following morning I went to the corner store for a bottle of wine and my temporary rosy world turned black. Mary, Chris, and Tim were in school and with just two children home it was easier for me to drink.

It was hard to drink and then try to pull myself together before Karl got home. Part of my insanity was actually believing that he didn't know. That I had fooled him. But it never lasted. Sooner or later I was passed out when he got home.

We argued the same old arguments. He told me I was drunk and I told him I wasn't drunk. I told him the neighbors were watching me and I was sick of it. He said he was going to have the Navy stop my allotment and through it all I kept right on drinking.

Mornings were dreadful. I had to get that first drink to get the children off to school. Sometimes I forgot to leave myself that morning drink and I shook so badly I'd have to run to the store and get a bottle while the kids were dressing.

Karl gave in to the situation and stayed away as much as he could. He came home only to see if the children were surviving. They were, because they were big enough now to take care of each other.

When I was too drunk to fix supper Chris and Mary would fry hamburgers or eggs and most of the time they turned out raw. Mary patched holes in the clothes and took care of the little ones.

I rarely ate, never took a bath, never combed my hair, and lost all touch with reality. For the next six months all I remember knowing was how to get my half-gallon bottles of wine. I hoarded, hid, and drank all the wine I could while making very feeble attempts to care for my children.

Soon I stayed in bed most of the time. Lady lay beside me on the floor. No matter what I did Lady knew nothing but love for me. If I had an hour in the morning without a drink she ran around happy. Then when I began again she would stay by my side—not in judgment, but waiting. Karl loved Lady, too, and I am certain that when he hit me she thought we were playing. If not, it was simply unbelievable to her.

100   I was in bed when someone knocked on the door.

"Who is it?" I yelled to the kids.

"It's the chaplain," Mary said.

I saw fire. "Tell him to go away. I don't want to see him."

Before I knew it, he was at the bedroom door and Lady was growling.

I grabbed Lady's choke chain. "Don't come any closer or I'll let her go."

"But your husband . . ." the blue uniform said.

"Get out! Get out of my house and my life!"

"But you're very ill."

"It I want to die it's none of your fucking business! Now get going before I turn this dog loose."

Lady showed her teeth and growled more. The chaplain left.

I decided, after that, to give in and if I died I would be happy and out of misery. The only catch was, I always seemed to wake up. I never died. It made me angry at God.

One evening Karl stayed home and we watched television, he with his beer and me with my wine.

"I can't see the tv," I said.

"Drink some more wine."

"Oh, I don't drink that much."

"Yeah?"

I stared at the television again. "Karl, I can't see. I'm going blind!"

"I wonder why? Oh, go to bed."

During the night I woke up and my belly was one solid pain. I moaned and fell out of bed. My whole body was writhing, twisting, and jerking. Karl lifted me back to bed. "You fool, you're killing yourself."

"Get me a doctor," I pleaded.

"I ought to let you lay there."

I overheard the doctor. "She's pretty far gone. I'll leave her some pills for the night but I would suggest you get her to a hospital tomorrow before she has another seizure."

When Karl left the next morning I pulled another bottle from under the ironing, drank some, and took the pills the doctor had left me. I could see a iittle better and my nerves were asleep again. That night another pain hit and it felt like a large lump pressing on my lower abdomen.

My God, it's labor pains! And I'm only eight months

pregnant! It must be dead . . . my baby must be dead, I thought.

I told Karl and he rushed me to the hospital. The doctors were angry at me for not having any prenatal checkups and I'm sure my physical condition was more than obvious.

"Have you been around any contagious diseases lately?" the doctor asked as he was taking my history.

I remembered that Susan had just gotten over chicken pox and when I told him he called the nurses who hurried me into an isolation room. They helped me undress and get into bed and then said they were putting a "No Admittance" sign on the door. Gowns and masks were to hang outside for anyone who had to come in. The door closed. I was alone—all alone.

I felt my forehead—wet. I felt my belly—flat. I looked around the barren room. The withdrawals from alcohol had started and the labor pains were tearing at my belly. I was shaking, thrashing, and sweating.

"Oh God, let me die. I can't stand it. Please, dear God, I want to die—now!"

I rang the buzzer over and over and each time the nurse checked me she said, "You're not dilating enough."

Through oceans of tears I begged, "Please give me some pills. Please, I can't stand it."

"I'm sorry. I can't do that." And she'd close the door again.

My brain was bursting wide open and everything was falling out. "Help me, someone. Help me!"

I turned over and saw a religious paper on the bedstand. I picked it up and tried to read the prayers. I couldn't so I threw it on the floor.

"Dear God in heaven, please help me. I'll never drink again, if you'll just help me."

My nerves were shattered and the labor pains were unbearable. Still, there was no escape. It was hours before I went to the delivery room.

"Your son weighs three pounds," the doctor said. "We have him in an incubator."

I was just coming to when I heard the doctor's words.

"Is he going to live?"

"I'm sure he is."

20

I left Steve in the hospital until he weighed the required five pounds. Two weeks later when I was able to bring him home I was aware of having a tiny five-pound life in my hands and knew that I would have to be very careful. My intentions were always good.

The other children were happy with their new brother but looked at me with suspicious eyes. They made me nervous and angry. "Stop looking at me. I'm all right!" I'd yell.

Karl loved all the children. I was sure of that but I felt it was only when he didn't have anything else to do. Drinking with his buddies took precedence over everything and when he was home it was a contest of saying to me, "See how I really care and what a bum you are." The Navy allowed him to be a married bachelor. And my drunkenness was a good excuse to stay away.

He told me he was being transferred to a ship in Long Beach and if he had the money he would come home on weekends. I was relieved, as usual.

With Karl's departure and absolutely nothing to look forward to, I became a walking zombie. Every morning I made my trek to the corner store and spent the rest of the day staggering hopelessly around the apartment trying to take care of things. Somehow Steve was surviving until one day the woman across the hall came to see him.

"In there," I said, trying to act sober.

Steve was lying face down in the bassinet, his head in the pillow and the blankets over his head.

The woman screamed, "What's the matter with you? This baby is smothering!"

Thick tongued, I shouted back, "That's my baby and you leave him alone!"

The woman had Steve in her arms. I staggered toward her and she knocked me down on the bed.

"You give me my baby and get out of here."

"You damn fool. You'd better straighten out and take care of these kids. You almost killed this one!"

"Get out of here and don't come back."

The woman put Steve on the bed and walked out.

Was she going to turn me in? What was I going to do?

I heated a bottle on the stove, swayed back and forth trying to change Steve's diaper, and almost dropped him walking to a chair. All during his feeding I sipped on my glass of wine.

103

Chris came in for lunch. "Are you okay, Mom?"
"I'm okay, Chris."
"Here's a letter that was in the mailbox. Here, let me take the baby."

Chris finished feeding Steve and put him back in the bassinet. I read my letter.

December 15, 1955—9:50 E.S.T.

Dear Children:

I am back in the State Hospital. Your mother and Howard moved in with me when Doctor John died. Howard was drinking heavily and they decided to take a trip to Buffalo. Howard died in your mother's arms in a motel room. She insisted on an autopsy and no one understood how he lived so long. His insides were eaten up with demon alcohol. I feel very sorry for your mother. She went into a deep depression and stayed in bed for three weeks. Wouldn't even eat much. I am helpless here in the hospital. My ward is so hot. These old ladies can't stand fresh air and I nearly suffocate.

I have no idea what they have done with all my nice things. They sold my cherry drop-leaf table and all of Doctor John's hunting guns. I can't worry as long as there is enough money to keep me going.

Remember one thing Nancy—you come from good stock. I know you will teach your children the valuable things in life—which is not money. We did our best by you with all the problems you gave us. Your mother was a trial too. She always did exactly what she wanted to do. Sometimes I admired her for it but I always had your Grandfather to contend with.

I have read many things over the years and tried to keep informed about politics and other issues. Did you know that Susan B. Anthony, a great reformer, went to jail in Rochester for her march on the right to vote?

Jimmy is doing well. He is in Medical School and will be a Medical Illustrator. His life has not been easy either. I enjoy my radio—especially the ball-games. There is little left for me to do as my eyesight is failing. Please try and write to me all about the children and you. I can get the nurse to read it to me. I hope you can read this scribbling.

I am hopeful that the world will someday find a way to peace. And one thing is certain: "God has a womb!" And I won't mind going home.

Love to you and the children, Grandma

P.S. I was committed as an "Incompetant Person."

I wept, took another glass of wine, and went to sleep.

* * *

Karl came home for Christmas and the Welfare Department stopped by with mended toys and a basket of food. I bought more wine. I was angry that someone had told the welfare people that we were a needy family but I was glad for the chance to spend the little money I had on wine. I always rationalized that eighty-two cents was not very much money for a fifth of wine and after all I had it coming. I never counted the hundreds of half-gallons I bought. How I managed to weed out all that extra money is still a mystery to me. Of course we had nothing else.

In my brief moments of being sober I felt as though I had "guilt" stamped in big letters across my forehead. To think of the past was unbearable and there was no future.

Christmas morning Karl brought out a fifth of liquor and invited the people across the hall for a drink. The children were opening the presents that were under the skinny tree and I drank a waterglassful of liquor.

When the people left I was in a stupor and Karl was lecturing again. I heard only a faint voice, however, because things were happening to my body.

I looked at the walls and they were moving. I looked through a haze at the television. Faces. No one I knew. They faded away. Nothing would stay still. Everything moved in slow motion. Finally I put my head between my knees so as not to look. I was staring at the living room floor when it happened.

First it was stumps of trees covering the floor. Then they began to grow. They grew right through the floor and got bigger and bigger. The branches grew out and leaves appeared. I tried to open my mouth to speak, but could not. The entire living room was one solid mass of trees and through them in every corner and every branch, was Karl's mouth—moving—moving—moving. I blacked out.

Karl went back to Long Beach and Chris started giving me trouble. At ten years of age he was very aware of my problem.

"I'm running away, Mom." He started out the front door.

"Come back here, you goddamn little brat. I'm going to beat your butt off."

"I ran away for three days once, and you didn't even know I was gone!" he shouted.

"I'm going to call the police," I said.

"Go ahead, see if I care. I'll tell them all about you," he cried.

Chris ran out.

Oh my God, I couldn't even control my children. What was going to become of us?

The entire responsibility was too much for me to think about and that called for more wine.

Karl and I had lost everything we ever felt for each other when we were young. He managed to stay away. I would have welcomed someone taking my children. I could not handle anything and all I wanted to do was die.

Karl had left the car and when Chris returned later that night I asked him if he thought going to a drive-in movie would help. Something in my mixed-up mind made me think if I did something for my children it would help. Chris agreed that it might.

I put their pajamas on, took my bottle of wine, and drove to the drive-in—drunk. I drank all through the movie. I remember nothing about the movie or how we all got home. After they were all in bed my mind raced and raged.

There was no point in torturing this family any longer. I would simply have to kill all of us.

That was when I turned on the gas.

How I ever got the gas turned off I'll never know but standing in front of the mirror the next morning and seeing myself for the first time in many years did something to me. I walked out of the bathroom, put on a robe, walked right out the front door, and knocked on the door across the hall.

The woman who had hollered at me about Steve answered the door.

"Would you please call Alcoholics Anonymous?"

106   "I'd be glad to."

21 Within half an hour two women arrived. I nervously asked them to sit down.

"I'm Kate, and I'm an alcoholic," the first one said.

"I'm Nancy," I said.

"I'm Betty and I'm an alcoholic," the other woman remarked.

I couldn't sit down so I paced, wrung my hands, and looked again at these two clean women who were telling me they were alcoholics. What a farce, I thought.

"We've both felt just like you do now and we'd like to help you."

My body was screaming for the wine I knew I had left in the bottle. "I have to have a drink."

"Put it off for a few minutes and maybe we can help," Kate said.

"I'm so nervous. I can't."

"I felt the same way for years," Betty said.

No one had ever felt this bad. What did they know, anyway?

They both told their stories and how they finally kicked alcohol. They told me I had a disease and it was called alcoholism and it was nothing to be ashamed of. They said I could try not drinking a minute at a time and eventually I would come down and be done with it. All during their conversation I kept thinking about the wine but suddenly a great feeling of warmth hit me and I knew I was no longer alone.

The longer they stayed the sicker I got and my mind went from one thing to another. First wanting help and then craving the wine. They kept right on talking. I tried not to shake but it didn't work. I was really getting worse. I wanted them to leave but they stayed.

"I've never gone this long without a drink. I can't stand it."

"We'll stay and help you get through it."

"It's no use. I'm no damn good. You're wasting your time on me. Look at this mess. Why don't you just let me die?"

"What have you got to lose by trying, once? We've been here for almost an hour and you haven't had a drink yet."

The baby started to cry.

"Excuse me. I have to change the baby and feed him."

Kate followed me into the bedroom. "I'll help you."

Dirty clothes were piled in the corner, halfway up the wall. There were no sheets on the bed. The bassinet was clean enough but a strong urine smell came from the baby. I opened the dresser drawer and frantically searched for a clean diaper.

"Goddamn it! There's no diapers."

Kate was holding the baby. "Come on, now, we can find something. A clean towel or napkin?"

"I guess so. Out in the closet maybe. I don't know."

When Kate put Steve down on the bed I looked at him and cried. "I can't take care of you. I can't take care of any of you. It's too much. I can't do it. I'm sick. I just can't do it!"

Kate returned. "See here, I found a nice clean napkin."

I went to fix a bottle and she changed Steve. I pulled a can of milk from the shelf, opened it, filled a baby bottle halfway with milk and the rest of the way with water from the spigot. I put in a little Karo syrup and heated the bottle in a pan of water on the stove. All the while I was wiping away tears with my arm.

I handed the bottle to Kate who fed Steve and I felt as though I would die.

The sweat clung to my cheeks. "Look at me! One small job and I fall apart."

"You're doing fine," Betty announced.

Somehow I believed her a little bit. They mentioned taking me to an AA meeting and I emphatically told them I wouldn't think of going out. But I could tell they were going to be patient.

After Steve was back in his bassinet they got up to leave. "We're leaving our phone number in case you need us and the woman across the hall said she'd watch your children when we take you to the meeting."

I thanked them for coming and closed the door. I went to the bathroom, held a cold washcloth to my face, and once again looked in the mirror. I tried to pull a comb through my hair. It was no use. I walked around the apartment looking at the mess. All the dirty clothes, the sticky kitchen floor, the food-stained furniture, and the spots on the wooden floors where David had wet through his diaper. The old washer sat in the kitchen. When I lifted the lid I found it full of dirty, smelly diapers that hadn't even been rinsed out first. It was so full that it had stopped working. I went to the bedroom and got the wine I had saved. I carried it to the kitchen and set it in the sink. I had not taken a drink and my body was one solid pain. I finally fell on the floor and writhed and cried. I looked up at the wine bottle and it looked directly back at me. I couldn't imagine what I was going to do next.

I pulled myself up to the sink and drank water like someone dying of thirst. Abruptly I grabbed the wine, put it in the cupboard, and stood erect.

I didn't know. I wondered if I had a chance. They had said "a minute at a time." What would happen if I took one drink? Ha . . .I'd be drunk again. I couldn't do it. I couldn't stop shaking. Maybe just one? God, how many times had I said that? I couldn't drink and I couldn't stop. But I thought I'd try. Oh, God, I'd try.

The front door opened. Chris walked in and behind him, Mary and Tim. They were home for lunch.

22

Chris looked at me and saw I wasn't drunk. Mary started making peanut butter sandwiches. "I don't think we have enough bread, Mom."

I got out my purse to see if I had any money left.

Anxiously Chris said, "I'll go to the store, Mom."

I searched until I found enough for bread. My hands were trembling, making it difficult to hold the purse.

"You're not drinking are you, Mom?" Chris asked.

"No, I'm not drinking."

"Oh, Mom."

I thought he was going to cry.

Tim, six, sat at the kitchen table waiting and then I saw my children. Torn jeans, worn-out tennis shoes. Mary's dress was entirely too long.

"Where's Susan and David, Mom?" Mary asked.

"Oh, I forgot. The lady across the hall watched them while the AA women were here. Will you go get them, Mary?"

Chris returned and they all sat down together to eat their sandwiches and drink their milk. I was too sick to sit and had to keep pacing.

"You look good, Mom," Mary said.

I hugged Mary. "Oh, honey, I don't feel very good. I'm very sick."

"We'll help, Mom," Mary said. They all nodded their heads in agreement.

The more I looked and listened to my children the more frightened I was about not drinking. The young ones were laughing about kid things and somehow that made me mad.

If they'd only known how sick I was they'd have shut up. This place! Cleaning it wouldn't improve it much. Oh, I was so Goddamn sick.

The three older children were ready to go back to school. They said goodbye and I could see in their eyes they didn't expect very much from me. Every day they sat in the classroom, worrying about me and the younger children, and trying to pay attention to the teacher. Would I forget to feed the baby? Would I watch David and Susan? Or would I possibly get drunk and set the house on fire?

I tried to wash David and Susan and put them down for a nap. They both got in their beds because even at two and three they knew how violent I could get. When

I was drunk I made them go to bed a lot and if they didn't I spanked them.

When I thought I had them settled, the baby started to cry. I felt so weak, I was afraid to pick him up. With a great deal of effort I managed to change him and feed him another bottle. Even after he drank all the milk he still cried and the crying was making me more nervous. Picking him up and rocking him didn't seem to help.

David and Susan were not asleep. They were laughing and playing in their beds. The wine flashed through my mind again.

If I took a drink I wouldn't have to think. But I had to try this time. Why didn't he stop crying?

I yelled at David and Susan, "Shut up, Goddamn it!"

I went back to baby Steve and turned him on his tummy. He still cried. I picked him up, sat on the bed, and rocked him. He still wouldn't stop crying. I put him back in the bassinet and by this time my nerves were like razor blades with all the edges hanging out of my body. I flew into a rage, picked Steve up again, held him up by his tiny arms, shook him furiously, and screamed, "Stop that! Goddamn it, stop it or I'll kill you!"

Instantly I put him back in the bassinet, ran out of the bedroom, sat rigidly on a chair, held my hands together, and begged for help.

"Someone, please help me before it's too late. Oh, God, what have I done? Where is Karl to help me?"

I sat like a stone until Steve fell asleep. By then David and Susan were asleep too. I had to move. I couldn't sit there all day. One by one I took the diapers out of the washer and rinsed them out in the toilet. I picked up dirty clothes, put sheets on the bed, and washed the dishes. In order to sustain myself, I chewed on white crackers. Late that day I called Kate and she persuaded me to go to an AA meeting. The woman across the hall said she would be more than willing to babysit.

Kate left me off in front of my apartment after the meeting. "Do you feel better?"

"Oh, yes! I didn't have any idea there were so many people with the same problem."

"Call me when you want to go again."

When I got into the apartment I thanked the woman from across the hall for staying with the children and when she left I crawled into bed with some literature I'd been given at the meeting. For a week I cleaned and polished the apartment and spent time listening to my children. One evening after they had all gone to bed a great feeling of loneliness came over me. I thought it was time to write a letter.

Dear Karl:

I don't know how to begin this letter as I realize how disgusted you are with me. Please try to understand. I am finally able to admit that I have a serious drinking problem. That is not easy. I know this will come as a surprise to you because you have been trying to make me get sober for a long time. As I understand it, the people closest to us can't help. I have met some very nice people and they're all sober alcoholics. They are going to help me stay away from drinking. So far it's been one week. Maybe that doesn't sound like much to you but it is a very long time for me. The first two days I thought I was going to die. Now I feel a little better. The children are very happy and also helping me. I know the last ten years have been hell for you and I want to say I'm sorry. That is what we call making amends. I understand the only real way to make amends is to stay sober. I am hoping and praying that I will be able to do it. If you would like to come home next weekend and see us we would be very happy. Is there any way that you could possibly send me some extra money so I can pay some bills. You haven't sent any in such a long time. I have cleaned up the apartment the best I could and will be looking forward to a letter from you. Just give me one more chance—please. I am trying. Oh God, Karl, please be on my side . . . just this once.

Love, Nancy

It was six weeks after I wrote the letter that Karl announced in his letter that he would be coming home. I turned the radio on and danced.

What would he think? I wondered if he'd like me.

The day Karl was to arrive, the apartment, such as it was, was cleaner than it had ever been. I had received my allotment, paid some bills, bought the children a few clothes at Sears, and brazenly bought myself a sexy housecoat.

While we waited for Karl I remembered all the times he had gone away and come home and how different this was going to be. Like a honeymoon. I had not taken a drink for seven weeks and the whole world was new.

I looked in the mirror, combed my long hair again, tried to keep the kids quiet, and waited.

"Daddy, Daddy," Mary cried.

Tall Karl in his uniform stood in the door. The children swarmed around him and he kissed them all.

"There. Now let me see your mother a minute."

I stood there—clean, sober, healthy—in my new green housecoat. I guess he didn't believe what he saw. He stared at me, ran his hand over his crewcut, pulled in his belly, raised his head, and sarcastically said, "And who are you waiting for—another one of your lovers?"

I was dumbfounded. "Karl, what are you talking about?"

"You didn't get that fancied up for me!"

I walked toward him. "Aren't you going to kiss me?" Unbelieving, he casually bent down and kissed me. "That" smell again. I knew immediately he had been drinking.

I couldn't allow myself to panic. He wasn't the one with the problem—I was. But why did he have to come home with that stuff on his breath when I was trying so hard?

I restrained myself.

"Well, how do I look?"

"Different. I'll say that."

"Oh Karl, it's so wonderful. I feel so good. You'll never know what those people have done for me."

"Well, I'm glad someone could. I've been trying long enough."

"Aren't you happy for me?"

"Sure, but how many times have we been through this before?"

"You sound like you don't want me to stay sober."

"Please, Nancy. Ten years of the same thing, the same promises, the same messes. What do you want me to think?"

"Okay. Let's not talk about it."

As the evening wore on, we got a little more comfortable. Karl hadn't said much and I really wondered what he was thinking.

115

I couldn't stand being without sex any longer and I went right to Karl and kissed him, passionately. He took my hand and we went to the bedroom.

23 Nine months passed. I continued to feel good, kept my house in order, and turned into a real perfectionist. My children blossomed but caring for them, sober, was not easy. Drunk, I hadn't noticed things. Sober, I noticed everything. It was hard on them. Karl managed to come home, occasionally, and tried to act normal. His resentment showed, though.

He drank when he wanted to and went out when he chose. I needed him and tried to tell him but he kept insisting that I was the one with the problem.

Reality was seeing life as it was and I hated what I saw in my life—Navy life. I reflected on all the places we'd lived and the lack of money. "The Navy comes first" was a statement that haunted me. I knew it had been true. I wondered why I had stayed, or where I fit in, if I did at all.

Maybe I could go to work? I wasn't ready for a drafting job. I had to get well first. It would give us more money and make life easier. No. I would have to pay a fortune for a babysitter. It wouldn't even pay me to try. What was life all about, anyway? I was sure Karl wasn't going without sex in Long Beach. I felt like the only person in the whole world that didn't drink. Damn it! I had to put that out of my mind.

* * *

It was cold and raining very hard and all the children were in our tiny apartment screaming and fighting.

"For God's sake, watch television," I yelled.

"It's acting funny, Mom," Chris said.

I tried to adjust it and it went off completely.

"I'll go across the hall and call the repair man."

When I came back they were screaming and fighting and crying.

"Stop it, damn it! Read books or something."

The walls were closing in on me.

"Can we go out in the rain?" Susan asked.

"No, you can't go out in the rain!"

"When's the man coming to fix the tv?" Tim chimed.

"In half an hour."

I ran into the bedroom, slammed the door, and burst into tears.

My nerves were shot. I wanted just one drink. The Goddamn prison I was in was driving me to madness. I worked so hard and I got nothing.

The repair man fixed the television and the craving went away for a while—at least until later that evening when the terrible loneliness hit again.

Those awful stories I heard in AA. I'd never been locked up or in jail. I was different. I was the one that said I was an alcoholic and if I chose to say I wasn't, I could do that too. I was a free soul and certainly one beer wouldn't hurt me. I'd control my drinking. I wouldn't drink until after seven in the evening. Then I'd have two beers and no more. I was really not like those alcoholics. I could be a social drinker. I knew I could.

When I made the decision to get a six-pack of beer a great feeling of exhilaration came over me. It was a passion close to sexual contact. I was so excited knowing that once more I would feel mellow and be able to escape into my dreams and fantasies. It was more precious than anything I'd ever known. I walked to the store.

How wonderful it would be to sit and drift into lightness and gaiety with no worries and no guilts. And besides I had really done a fantastic job with my family. Everyone said so. Now I wanted something for me—just me.

In the store I had a twinge of guilt.

People bought beer every day and thought nothing of it. I was just being silly.

I hurried home with my treasure and put it in my bedroom closet so the children wouldn't see it. I was determined to be a "social drinker." After seven I stood in the closet, quietly opened the first can of beer, wrapped a sock around it, and stepped way back into the closet to drink it.

"I knew I could be a social drinker."

I had my two cans of beer without the children catching me and went to bed feeling very proud. In the morning I felt even more proud.

I had done it! Really done it! I wasn't an alcoholic. God, I hated that word. It sounded awful.

I fed the children, got them off to school, and sat down with a cup of coffee. About ten, I felt it. A sickish feeling in my stomach. I put the cracked coffee cup down and rushed around making beds. I kept saying to myself that it couldn't be happening.

I did know it and it was the compulsion. I knew it better than I knew my own name. The two cans of beer had set up the physical compulsion for more. My body was craving more alcohol. I tried to shake it off but the hangman would not leave. He tied the knot in my stomach and it got tighter and tighter. I dusted the wooden arms, the television, the end table. I washed the dishes, the clothes, and Steve. The noose was complete.

Somehow I stuck to the promise I'd made myself but when the clock read seven I ran and got the beer, opened the can in front of my frightened children, and gulped. Soon the other cans were empty and I was on my way to the store for a bottle of wine.

I couldn't look at my children because all I saw on their little faces was terror. It didn't matter. My jangled nerves were asleep.

One doctor had told me that the pain was my liver. I had also heard someone at AA say that your liver heals up faster than any other part of your body, if you don't put alcohol in it. I knew I could fool the doctor so I became a periodic drinker. I had to give my liver a chance to stay well.

Karl came home and I convinced him I was not an alcoholic.

"I told you you could do it. I never did understand why you couldn't have a few beers and stop. But you always had to get smashed before you quit."

"I've been doing just what you said—having a few beers and stopping. Honest I have."

"That's good. I didn't like you hanging around with all those jailbirds anyway."

We sat at the kitchen table drinking our beer.

"Are you ready to move again?" he asked.

"You mean we're going to move out of this mess?"

"Yep. Permanent duty in San Diego."

"After fifteen years. Maybe we could rent our old house?"

"Maybe."

It didn't happen that way. We couldn't find a landlord that would rent to a family with six children and a Doberman pinscher. The only place available was—a quonset hut!

My drinking got worse and the arguments with Karl more frequent. I still sobered up for a week at a time but it was getting harder and harder to stay away from alcohol.

One time I thought I was sicker than usual and I went to the hospital for a checkup.

"I'm so nervous, doctor. I can't sleep or anything."

"Do you have children?"

"Six."

"Six? No wonder you're nervous. Here's a prescription for some pills that should help."

It wasn't long before I figured out the pills were tranquilizers. They were beautiful. They stopped the shakes instantly.

From then on I made regular trips to the hospital to get my prescription refilled at the pharmacy. The pills saved me when I wasn't drinking. Some of the people in the quonsets were taking pills too and I borrowed all I could from anyone I could and stashed them away like a squirrel preparing for winter. Hiding and taking pills became just as much of an obsession as alcohol. Now it was one or the other or both.

The children all broke out with impetigo and the Navy doctor said it was from the dirt around the quonsets. For two weeks Karl and I had to bathe each one separately, dry them with separate towels, and put salve on each sore.

"Karl, we've got to get out of here!"

"And just where do you suggest we go?"

"I don't know but we have to find a decent place for these kids."

"Well, when you come up with something, let me know."

Word was passed around the quonsets that the admiral was coming by for his weekly inspection. That morning I began my day with three cans of beer and about eleven I saw the admiral approaching my hut. Ten people trailed along behind him. WAVEs, ensigns, lieutenants. When he got right in front of my door I stepped out onto the tiny wooden porch.

"Admiral, would you mind stepping in here a minute?"

"Certainly."

The aides looked shocked. Who was this peon who had the nerve to speak to the admiral and even invite him in? They gathered tightly around the tiny porch. The door remained open.

"Admiral, my husband has been in the Navy fifteen years. Is this the way his family has to live? Look at the dirt out there. Have you ever tried to live in a place where the cockroaches were winning? We just spent two weeks trying to heal our children from impetigo. The Navy doctor said it was from all this dirt and their playground is the drainage ditch! To tell you the truth, I'm sick of it!"

"Well, we'll just have to see what we can do about it, then. We're fixing up some duplexes and I'm sure we can get you into one soon."

"Thank you."

"You'll be hearing from me," he said as he walked out.

"Goodbye, Admiral."

"Goodbye."

The aides were writing on pieces of paper as fast as they could, and looking at the number on our hut.

Several days later Karl came rushing in. "Get ready, we're going to look at a new house. The admiral himself called me to his office today. He even sent his boat to pick me up on the ship. I thought I was in serious trouble. Why didn't you tell me what you'd done?"

"I wanted to surprise you."

At last I had a say in our affairs and I felt really good.

Mary watched the younger children while Karl and I went to look at our new house. The building had been a two-story, four-apartment dwelling. The Navy had made one unit out of the two middle apartments, just for large Navy families. Consequently it had two baths, four bedrooms, one large kitchen, and an enormous living room. I couldn't believe it. It was carpeted throughout and had real overstuffed furniture. It was elegant.

"Karl, can you believe there will be enough room for everyone? And grass outside—honest-to-God grass!"

"Yeah, it's nice."

"Nice? It's beautiful!"

I carefully sat down on the new couch. "I just can't really believe it."

I got up, closed the front door, walked toward Karl, and put my arms around him. "We'll make it this time, Karl. I know we will."

He pushed me away. "We'd better."

At our new home, the children ran from room to room and up and down the stairs. For once I heard real laughter from them and I was momentarily happy.

When we were all settled, Karl and I made more beer.

121

I felt safe and secure with the beer and the pills I had hidden. It wasn't long before I was adding wine to my list of securities, hiding it in the ironing and under the mattress.

I had to maintain. I'd do the dishes and fix the meals and Karl would never find out.

I tried control and in a couple of months alcohol was dictator. Not only did Karl and the children know but the entire neighborhood knew. During the day I would go from house to house trying to find a Navy wife that would drink with me. Most of them didn't want anything to do with me. Thelma was one that took pills so once in a while she would let me hang around her house. She also slipped me pills now and then.

Karl was ready to kill me, he was so frustrated.

"Why in the hell don't you stay in the house? Bad enough my shipmates know, but now all the neighbors know too. Don't you care anything about your children?"

"Don't you? You're gone every night, we don't do anything, and this Goddamn house is like living in a zoo."

"I was going to take you to a picnic Saturday, but how can I take you anywhere when you're drunk all the time?"

"A Navy picnic?"

"Yes. A picnic on the beach. The kids would love it."

"I'll straighten up if you'll take us."

"We'll see when Saturday gets here."

"I'll do it. I mean it. We'll all go to the picnic."

I did sober up and we did go to the picnic.

There were at least fifty couples on the beach. A lot of the men were playing volleyball and the women were all huddled together watching the children. Some of the men were cooking inch-thick steaks over a pit next to four kegs of beer. Some of the men were very drunk and many steaks ended up in the sand. The food had all been brought from the ship.

I really wanted a beer badly. I called to Karl, "Can I have one can of beer?"

He came over to me and said, "Don't start that!"

"Karl, everyone's drinking."

"Not you!"

"I'm kinda shaky, Karl. Just one—I promise."

He pulled my arm. "Come on, I'll take you body surfing in the ocean. That'll make you feel better."

"Who will watch the children?"

"They'll be all right. The other women will watch them."

"Please. I can't."

He kept pulling me along. "It'll help you. Get your blood circulating."

There was no choice left. I had to go in the big surf. Karl wouldn't give up and I was truly afraid of him. He went ahead of me, diving into the big waves and coming up again.

"Come on out further," he shouted.

"Give me time. I'm coming."

Slowly I made my way out to the big waves.

"Now dive in one of them and let it take you."

I did and underneath the water with the wave pouring over me, I knew how weak I really was.

These waves could kill me, I realized.

When the wave took me to shore, I stood up and saw Karl motioning for me to come out again.

I'd have to try once more. Oh, God, I was scared.

I came up out of the next wave and was face to face with Karl.

He grinned and pushed me under. "Try it again!"

The water swashed around in my mouth and I fought to come up. Every time I made it, he pushed me under again.

"Karl, stop it! Stop it!" I screamed. "Let me go!"

He pushed me under again and I tried desperately to swim toward shore. I knew in a flash that the waves wouldn't kill me but Karl would.

The last time I came up I was far enough away from Karl to get to the beach.

He yelled, "What's the matter, can't you take it?"

I got back to my blanket, lay flat on my belly, and tried to get my breath. I turned over onto my back.

Dear God, what was the matter with me? I was so sick.

Tears ran down the sides of my face.

24

Our lovely new home turned into a boxed-in skid row. The children were ragged and trying to take care of each other and Karl came home only occasionally to check on them. Sometimes he bought groceries. When I got my allotment, I bought a few groceries and liquor and when I ran out of money I borrowed from the neighbors. Every morning I walked to the liquor store to get my day's supply and as the months wore on and the money ran out I settled for cheap wine.

Karl would not let me have the car and went so far as to take my driver's license and all my identification out of my billfold. To add to my fears, Jimmy wrote that Mother was dying of cancer.

"I should go home, Karl."

"Yeah, you'd look cute. You couldn't stay sober long enough to get on the bus. Besides, we don't have any money."

I took another drink and Karl grabbed the wine bottle and slapped me. "You drunken sot!"

I passed out again and when I came to, Karl was gone and the children were in bed.

I had to stop drinking. Oh, my God, I couldn't stand it. I'd stop drinking in the morning. But I'd tried a million times before. What the hell was I going to do?

That night I lay in bed trying to sleep. Suddenly a face appeared on the wall. Then the whole body of Jesus Christ appeared in a white cloud. I tried to get up and couldn't move. Jesus held out his hand. I cried, "I can't reach!" I passed out.

*   *   *

The months that followed were one long nightmare. My addiction had reached the point of no return. I looked, acted, and felt completely hopeless.

"If I could just die. Why don't I die?" I thought.

I kept my allotment away from Karl, knowing this was my only link with life and the thing that kept me going—booze. I opened a checking account and had the Navy send my allotment directly there. As the days passed everything was obscure and vague and I knew nothing about what was going on around the house. I drank so much in the daytime and took such precautions to hide bottles and pills that my entire life was my addiction.

124

Every morning was the same. I walked to the kitchen and stood there shaking.

"I can't go through another day like this! I can't drink this morning. I've got to stop—somehow."

The children came down for breakfast and I put the cereal on the table.

Maybe just one would stop the shakes. No, it would only start all over again. I couldn't stop shaking.

Chattering children on their way to school, Steve and Susan playing on the living room floor, and all the voices merged in my ears.

"Just one."

Of course, after the one it was too late and I was on my way to the liquor store, leaving the two little ones alone. My belly hurt so badly that I had to hold it and walk stooped over. The store wasn't far but to me the distance was like the Mojave Desert.

When I get home and get a drink I'll be all right; to-morrow I can stop, I thought.

Somehow Karl got us through Christmas of 1957. He provided some presents and a tree. It was vacation time for the children and one night when Karl had to stay on the ship I saw the car parked out in front. I knew where there was an extra key and decided to take the children downtown to see Santa Claus.

Santa was at one of the big hotels and when I piled all the scrubby children into the car, I was very drunk. I got lost and ended up on a very dark street.

"Mom, look out!" Chris bellowed.

It was too late. I felt a thud and saw a woman flying through the air. The children shrieked, "Mommy, Mommy, you hit a lady!"

They cried and I sobered up for a minute, got out, went over to the woman, and picked her up.

"Are you all right?"

The woman said nothing, got up, brushed herself off, and stood, shaking. She was about sixty-five and I soon knew she couldn't speak English. I quickly opened my purse, got out an old stubby pencil, wrote my name down and gave it to her. She still didn't speak. She took the paper and walked away. The children were sobbing and I knew a policeman would show up any minute.

No one came. I had thrown the woman about twenty-five feet and I was petrified. The enthusiasm about Santa was gone but since we had come to see him I was determined we would. I got to the hotel, parked the car, and the children said they didn't want to go in.

"Mom, we look too grubby to go in a place like that." Chris said.

"You'll go in! What difference does it make how you look? You're as good as anyone else."

I, in my wine-spotted housedress and torn black coat, headed the group. I walked right up to the desk. "Where's Santa Claus?"

The man replied, "Lady, he's gone. It's December 30th."

I took Steve and Susan and rushed out of the hotel. The others hurried along behind.

By some miracle I never heard from the woman again.

When we got home Karl was waiting. He had tried to call the house and when there was no answer he knew something was wrong. I went right to bed, pulled out another bottle, took a drink, and lay back. Then I saw Karl coming toward me.

"You slut. The kids told me what happened. I hope they lock you up for life."

"Me too," I muttered.

Karl pulled me out of bed and hit me. "How dare you? I'll sober you up for life."

I yelled and screamed and tried to fight him off but he raged and hit me harder. Suddenly I was tumbling down the stairs. Blood trickled out of my head and onto the floor. I struggled to get up and finally made it.

"My head, oh my head," I moaned.

I went to the mirror and saw blood running down my face. "Karl, take me to the hospital! Hurry!"

Karl stood over me, straight and tall. "I'm not taking you anywhere."

"Please, Karl, I'm sure I need stitches."

"I don't give a damn what you need."

Mary came to me with a cold towel and Karl stormed out the front door.

"It's okay, Mom, it doesn't look so bad."

"Oh, Mary, help me to bed, please."

Mary sat beside my bed.

"Please, Mary, don't hate me. Please, please."

"I don't hate you, Mom."

"Would you hand me a drink of wine? It's under the bed."

"Why don't you go to sleep, Mom?"

"I will if I can just have one drink. I need a drink."

Mary got the bottle for me.

"Please, please say you don't hate me. I love you so much. I'm so sick."

"Just try to go to sleep, Mom."

"Are the kids all right? Have they eaten?"

"Yes, Mom, everything's all right. Please go to sleep."

"Stay with me, Mary, please. I'm afraid to be alone. Please help me."

"I'm right here, Mom."

I guess Mary left.

Rainbows filled my bedroom. Jesus appeared on the wall and then left. In the corner of the ceiling was a gigantic black spot and it grew webs. More and more of them kept coming at me. I pulled the covers over my head.

I couldn't let them get me. They couldn't get through the rainbows.

Bigger and bigger webs, filling the whole room and touching my bed. I closed my eyes tightly and then peeked again. The rainbows were gone. I let out a terrified scream that brought Chris running.

"I saw it, Chris, I saw it."

"There's nothing there, Mom. Now go back to sleep."

"Stay with me, Chris."

"Mom, there's nothing I can do."

I shut my eyes and tried to sleep. The clock read three o'clock. I moved my body into the womb position and tried to be still. It seemed as though hours had passed but when I looked at the clock again it was three minutes after three. I got up, went downstairs, and called AA. They refused to come, saying the same thing as always. "We can't help you until you want to help yourself."

The days dragged on. Each one the same.

I put Susan in for a bath, turned on the hot water, and reeled to my bedroom. Susan screamed and Karl ran and pulled her out of the bathtub. She was badly scalded and I wept while Karl applied burn ointment.

"What the hell have you done now?"

127   Bed became the only place left, and I stayed there

with the wine and pills I had left, totally oblivious to the children.

I crawled downstairs and reached the telephone.

"Karl, come home home right now. I'm dying."

He was home in ten minutes. He went upstairs to the bathroom, and then stood there, far above me, at the top of the stairs. I was at the bottom, holding onto the banister.

He said, "How many times do you think I can leave my job for this nonsense?"

In his uniform, at the top of those stairs, he looked like Hitler. I looked at him, and with my eyes begged for understanding.

"Oh God, Karl, please."

"Look at you. Filthy, dirty mess. A nothing with a warped mind."

He carefully walked down each step to the bottom where I was. I stooped, in pain, beside him and felt like an insignificant ant.

"Karl, you've got to do something to help me. I've gone mad."

"What the hell do you want me to do?"

I got down on my knees and pulled at his pants. "Please, Karl, please, I'm losing my mind. I can't stop drinking. Do something. Anything."

"I can take you downtown to the Mental Health Office. If you sign some papers they'll help you."

"All right. I'll go. Just one more drink first."

"No more drinks. Get in the car—now."

"The children?"

"Since when do you worry about the children? You almost killed Susan in the bathtub and you hit Steve in the head with a croquet mallet."

"I what?"

"You heard me."

"I don't remember doing that."

"Get in the car."

Karl was whispering to the children and I managed to get into the car, somehow.

When we got to the door of the Mental Health Office I was ready to collapse and I wasn't sure I wanted to go in. But it was too late to change my mind. We went in and sat down. A man called us into his office to sign the papers. They said something about treatment but my brain was not functioning well. I signed.

Karl told me that he was taking me to a place that would give me the help I needed. I asked what place it was and he said it was a hospital.

"Are there bars on the windows?"

"No."

"If there's bars on the windows you won't make me go in, will you?"

"No."

"Promise?"

"Yes, yes."

25

We drove up in front of a building that looked like a hospital. I couldn't see any bars on the windows so I walked in, holding onto Karl.

By this time I was really sick. My knees were shaking and my nerves felt like a fingernail on a blackboard. I was doubly scared when I saw the rough-looking nurse who came to take my papers and me. Karl said goodbye and the buxom nurse led me to the showers.

"Take off your clothes and get in that shower. There's pajamas, slippers, and robe on the chair. Put them on," the nurse barked.

"Take a shower? I can't take a shower. I'm too sick. I'll fall."

"Honey, you have to take a shower so get in there."

Soon another nurse came to my rescue. The quiet nurse put her arm around me. "It's all right. I'll help you."

When I took off my clothes I was ashamed of all the black-and-blue marks on my body. Some were from Karl and others were from bumping into the furniture.

The quiet nurse helped me into the shower and held onto me while I rinsed off. I put the pajamas on and put my feet in the cotton slippers. I was afraid to say it out loud but I wondered why the slippers didn't match.

The nurse led me to the dayroom and then I saw it all. I looked at the windows. No bars—but heavy mesh wire that kept the patients from escaping.

"Where am I?" I asked the nurse.

"This is the Psychiatric Ward of the County Hospital." How could I have been so stupid?

There they all were—women walking, talking, chanting, rocking, singing, and one baptizing everyone with water from a tin cup. Suddenly I was sure I saw the back of Grandma's head with her hair hanging down.

I found a chair and sat down next to a young girl about eighteen.

"See that broad over there? She's a les."

"Is that right?"

"Yeah, sometimes this place gives me the willies."

"It's scary."

"What you in here for?"

"I'm trying to get help. I'm an alcoholic."

"Yeah? Well, they'll give you a bunch of pills, dry you out, and that's about it."

"What are you in here for?"

"Shootin' smack—they say. My fourth time in. What the hell do they know? The dirty rotten bastards say I don't know anything any more. Just 'cause I've screwed a few guys and had a baby. Let me tell you—that doc is the one."

She wiggled her body. "Called me in his office for an interview. Tried to screw me—honest. How's that grab you? Then when I told him to get lost he calmly said I had trouble forming my feminine mother role! That's what they always tell you. Goddamn men—if you don't do what they tell you to do they declare you insane!"

They brought the night meal to the big room and I took two bites of the cold meatloaf and pushed it aside. At about eight-thirty a nurse came and led me to a desk in the hall. She handed me something to drink.

"It's paraldehyde," the nurse said.

The smell was so horrible I couldn't get it past my nose, let alone drink it.

"It'll make you feel better."

"I'm sorry, I can't drink it."

She took me to my room. One bed, one nightstand, and a bedpan. Hanging from the sides of the bed were leather straps.

"What are those for?" I asked.

"In case you have DTs."

"Oh, I won't, I won't."

"You don't know. You're in pretty bad shape. Well, anyhow, here's some pills that will get you through the night."

The nurse walked out and closed the big heavy door with the one tiny square window. I heard the key turn in the latch.

"Nurse, nurse, what are you doing? You can't lock it!" I screamed.

The nurse peered through the small window. "Sorry, but it's the rules. Before this night's over you'll be glad it's locked."

I crawled into the high iron bed, covered myself with one sheet and one blanket, and curled up into a ball.

What was I doing here? I was not a criminal. Why did they lock me in? I was not insane. Oh God, why couldn't I stop shaking? There was no way out of here. I was a trapped animal. Oh, dear God!

All night the other women moaned, sobbed, and cried. I couldn't sleep at all. I heard the woman in the next room yelling, "If you don't take these goddamn straps off I'm going to piss the bed. Do you hear me, you goddamn jailers? Okay, I did, you sons-of-bitches. I pissed the bed."

Two days later I felt better and played cards with the other alcoholic women. During one game a nurse wheeled a patient into the dayroom in a wheelchair.

"I want all you alcoholics to take a good look at what can happen to you."

I was stunned. The woman in the wheelchair was green. Her whole body was bloated and her eyes were almost shut.

"This lady is dying of cirrhosis of the liver. And what's more, the men get even worse. Their penises swell up so big we can't get them in the bedpan and their urine turns to yellow syrup."

If the woman in front of me was conscious at all I thought the nurse was being very cruel.

The nurse turned to wheel the patient out. "Don't worry, she doesn't even know what I'm saying. She won't last two more days."

No one came to visit me and I knew nothing of the outside world. I was so terribly lonely. I needed love from someone. After five days I was taken to the psychiatrist's office to be interviewed. I saw the tape recorder on his desk.

He was a white-haired man about sixty. He put his hands behind his head and leaned back in his chair. He made me feel like he was God.

"Did you hit your son on the head with a croquet mallet?" he said sternly.

I was desperately trying to be calm and rational.

I have to say the right thing or I'll never get out of this place. I didn't remember hitting Steve but maybe I had.

I answered, "Yes, sir."

"Do you know that you can't drink?"

"Yes, sir. I'm never going to drink again."

"Do you know that your children will be taken away from you if you continue to drink?"

"Yes, sir."

132   "You're excused. Go out in the hall and wait until

they call you for court. I will make my recommendations and the judge will decide. He may want to send you to the state hospital for three months."

"Thank you, sir."

I was led to the bench in the hall to wait.

I wondered if that doctor drank. Where did he get all that power to decide people's fate? They weren't saying a thing about Karl and his drinking. I was so confused.

In the court I spotted Karl, the judge, and other people. They were sentencing mentally ill people? My God!

When they called my name, I stood up.

The judge spoke. "I have read your case. You are an alcoholic. This is your first time in here so I'm going to let you go home. Don't come back again."

He hit the table with his gavel and Karl came to take me home.

When we walked into the house I saw all the children's clothes ironed and hanging on the stairway.

"Who did all that?"

"I did," Karl piously answered.

We said no more. The next morning Karl left for work and the children left for school. Steve and Susan were playing in the backyard. I was alone. I was terrified. I walked to the front window in the living room. It had a screen on it. I put my hands high on the window, my face on the glass, and wept.

I was just as locked in as I had been in the psycho ward and I just knew I'd have to drink again.

26

I'd try. I just had to try not to drink.

A week later Karl brought home a bottle of gin and one of vermouth.

"I thought I might make myself a martini. I've had a rought week," he said.

"I've had a rough week too."

"Why do you always complain about something you're supposed to be doing anyway?"

"It's not easy, Karl, trying to take care of six kids."

He looked disgusted again and proceeded to fix his drink. I wanted one so badly I ached.

"Could I have one too?"

"Absolutely not."

"Why do you drink in front of me, then?"

"Quit complaining. I've told you before, you're the one with the problem—not me. This is my home and if I want to drink, it's my right."

"I could have just one and no more."

"You really believe that?"

"Of course. Look at me, I'm fine. There's no reason why we can't have one together. Why don't you try me, just once?"

I put the glass to my lips, sipped, and sighed. When it reached my stomach—instant warmth, immediate relief, and that beautiful glow. The noise of the children coming in for supper didn't even faze me.

After we fed the children we had a few more drinks and Karl began making love to me.

"Let's take the whole bottle upstairs and go to bed," he said.

We were both getting very drunk, and holding onto each other and the bottle we tottered upstairs.

When Karl handed me the bottle I gulped as much as I could and took off my clothes. I never remembered sexual intercourse when I was drunk and I know I never had an orgasm. I simply lay back and pretended I was enjoying it, mostly to please Karl so he would let me drink.

7:00 and Karl had gone to work. I jumped up and saw the empty gin bottle on the floor. I put my hand to my head.

I felt terrible. Not one drop left. I had to have a drink.

I started searching. I was certain there must be something in the house. I pulled all the ironing out of the closet—nothing. I looked under the mattress—nothing. I was frantic. I saw a bottle of perfume on the dresser and took a gulp. It did have alcohol in it. I ran downstairs and looked in all the cupboards—nothing. Did I have to drink more perfume to feed my addiction? Under the sink I found the vermouth and drank it.

In just two days the good deeds were over. The dishes piled up, the dust gathered, and the children were back to taking care of each other. When my allotment came, I stocked up on beer, wine, and liquor, stashing it everywhere. I sat in a stupor tipping the wine bottle and smoking cigarettes.

Time meant nothing—it was all the same. But it wasn't long before I knew I was pregnant.

It was my birthday and Karl walked in from work. He was on one of his nondrinking kicks to prove something to me.

"The least you can do is drink with me on my birthday."

"For God's sake, you're drunk now!"

"Come on, Karl, just one. It's my birthday."

"How'd you figure that out? You never even know when your children's birthdays are."

"You son of a bitch. You mean to tell me that you'll go out and drink with your buddies and you won't even drink with me?"

"Shut up, Nancy."

"Try and make me."

I lost control of everything in me and pushed Karl.

"Watch it now," he said.

I pushed him again. "Watch what?"

"Nancy, please."

I picked up the wine bottle and shoved in in his face. "Drink!"

He backed away. "Why don't you go upstairs and get some shoes on?"

I let loose and threw pots, pans, the iron, and furniture at him. He called the police and by the time they came I had calmed down.

I looked at the two giant policemen. "You mean he called the cops on me?"

"We'd just like to talk to you. Why don't you step out on the porch so the children won't hear?"

I was wearing short shorts and a sweater. I was barefooted. I staggered out on the porch and as quick as lightning they pulled my arms behind my back and handcuffed me. Tim ran out the front door and to the police car. "Here, Mom, here's your shoes. She can't go without her shoes," Tim cried to the two policemen.

I fought and screamed all the way to jail.

"You're not going to lock me up, you bastards. Take me home right now. You're real brave, handcuffing a woman. Now, Goddamn it, take me home."

The matron grabbed my arm and pushed me into a cell. Another woman sat on the top bunk looking very ill. I sat on the bottom bunk and held my head in my hands. I had to give up. I was in a tiny dirty cell with two bunks, one toilet, and a washbasin. The mattress was like tissue paper. The woman from the top bunk was now vomiting in the toilet.

"Shit, if I just had a drink," I muttered.

I couldn't sleep because the sweat was pouring off my body and I was dying for a drink. After four hours the matron took me to an office and fingerprinted me and then returned me to my cell.

Morning came and they let us all out to sit at a table and play cards. I sat with thieves, dope addicts, and alcoholics.

Why was I here? Because I was one of them!

I looked at all the women sitting around the table. Most of us were dirty and tough-looking but I felt a kinship like I had never felt before. I was sure their lives were as messed up as mine but what led us all to this point? Suddenly, I felt a great love for the other women because deep in my gut I knew none of us were really "Bad Women."

One of the women gave me a dime to make my one phone call. We were allowed only one and I knew Karl wouldn't bail me out.

Who could I call? Who would bail me out?

It was at that moment that I realized I didn't have one friend—not one.

The matron took me to the telephone and I nervously thumbed through the phone book. I had to think of someone. Thelma—yes, she would come and get me. My neighbor who had given me all the pills.

Thelma what? Oh, my God, what was her last name? Think, think, stupid! Thelma—Miller! That was it.

Thelma was more than happy to come after me. She paid the twenty-eight-dollar fine and I was released. On the way to the car I asked her if I could borrow three dollars. She gave it to me.

"Hey, maybe you'd better not drink for a while. I've got some pills here that you can get by on."

"Oh hell, Thelma, what's the difference? Pills, booze, it's all the same. I get just as sick on both."

I asked Thelma to let me out at the corner of my street and I just couldn't bring myself to go home. I walked to the corner bar with my three dollars. I ordered one beer after another and kept on sitting. Several men bought me beer and towards night I could hardly sit up on the stool. I really didn't care about anything and then the bartender said, "I want you to leave now."

"That's a fine way to treat a customer."

"Lady, you are very drunk. Would you please leave before I call the law?"

Two sailors offered to help me out and when we got outside they said they would buy a bottle and we could go to the beach.

On the beach, I faintly remember them laughing but everything was foggy. I asked them to hand me the bottle.

"Yeah, after you take your pants off."

They both screwed me and I got my drink. The next thing I knew was that they were gone. I started walking home and I couldn't find my house because Navy housing all looked alike. I tried to pull myself together and I finally found the right door. That's all I remember.

My fight to die was on and when I woke in the morning I was really angry that I hadn't died. "Dear God, please. I'm crying out to you once and for all—take me, take me this very moment. I can't stand this torture another minute."

I cried and laughed and stumbled around the house that morning, making feeble attempts to do housework. I heard a knock on the front door.

I couldn't let anyone in.

"Open up, lady," a man said harshly.

I opened the door.

"I'm from the FBI," he said, flashing his badge. "You'll have to come downtown with me."

137   Then I really started to shake. "For what?"

"They'll tell you downtown."

"I have six children. I can't leave them."

"That doesn't matter. You're under arrest."

"Will you give me a minute to get a neighbor to watch my children?"

"Okay, but hurry."

I ran out the back door to Thelma's house and she agreed to watch the children.

The man put me in the back seat of the black car and drove me to the Federal Building. They fingerprinted me, took mug shots, and told me to sit in a chair and wait.

They took me to the commissioner's office. The commissioner was a woman.

"Nancy, I have two checks here for one hundred dollars each that you wrote at the naval base. This was six months ago and you haven't had sufficient funds to cover them yet."

I was shocked. "I didn't write any checks."

"Is this your signature?"

I looked at the checks. The amounts and signature were scrawled. My mind raced.

"It's my writing and my check. But I don't remember. I don't remember anything!"

The commissioner had a very soft voice. "Do you know this is a felony?"

"Well, you see, I have a drinking problem and I'm going back to AA. I was sober once for nine months. Please give me a chance."

"I'm going to give you a chance to make restitution and I will put you on probation for three years. You seem like a fine woman and I know you'll do something about your problem."

"Oh yes, thank you, thank you."

The man in the dark suit drove me back home. I took a big drink of wine and continued wishing for death.

* * *

As many times as I tried to control my drinking, as many times as I stopped, and as many times as I tried not to start, it was to no avail. I was completely addicted to alcohol with tranquilizers and barbiturates as a sideline.

Nothing changed. Karl and I fought, he hit me, and I had open running sores on my body from not eating. The children walked around me and over me as though I was a flyspeck, and the house we lived in was a burning hell.

I couldn't stand the thoughts of withdrawal from alcohol. I didn't want the baby in my belly—I couldn't see the ones I had. And Karl—I never knew about him.

It was September 1958. I was five months pregnant and my stomach was flat. On the morning of the fifth I woke up sick, as usual. I had had hideous hallucinations the night before. Again, Jesus appeared on the wall. Only this time he was a woman with breasts. I tried to reach her and failed again.

No one wanted to bother with me. Karl would take care of the children.

I put on an old housedress, my torn black coat, and my old shoes. I picked up my purse with the checkbook in it and started walking down the street.

27

I walked to the shopping district and into a restaurant.
I sat down and ordered a bottle of beer.

"Can you cash a check?" I asked the waitress.

I was so scared. I knew I looked awful. I couldn't
remember when I had last bathed and it was impossible
to get a comb through my long hair.

"No, we don't cash checks here," the waitress answered.

"Will you call me a cab then?"

"Sure, lady."

I got into the cab, shaking furiously, really needing a
drink, but the driver didn't cash checks either.

"What am I going to do? I have to get a check cashed,"
I said.

Being very familiar with my situation, the cab driver
said, "I can take you to the marine base staff club.
They'll cash your check."

"That's fine," I said, trying to straighten my hair.

He drove me to the marine base and we got right
through the gate. He stopped in front of the club and I
told him to wait. The bar was lined with Marines, and I
quickly asked the bartender if he would cash a check.
My nerves were gone, and my voice was weak. A Marine
standing next to me said, "Hey, you look like you need
a drink."

"Yes, if you don't mind."

I swallowed fast to stop the hurting.

"I'll pay the cab fare," the Marine said.

"Oh, thank you. I'll pay you back when I get this
check cashed."

The Marine bought me several more drinks and I was
feeling a little better but getting drunk, again.

"Want to go some place else?" the Marine asked.

"Sure, any place you say."

We stopped at a liquor store for a bottle of gin and
then drove to a motel. The last thing I remember was
taking a big drink from the gin bottle. I blacked out.

Some time later my eyes slowly opened. I was in bed,
naked. The sheets were hanging on the floor, and there
was no one in the room with me. I raised myself up,
looked at my dirty body and fell back down.

A drink—I had to have a drink! Where was the bottle?
I had to find it!

It was in the corner on the bathroom floor. I picked
it up. Empty.

I ran a little water in it, swished it around, and drank it.

Where was I? What had happened? What did I do? Where were my children? Why couldn't I have died a long time ago?

I felt very odd.

I ran my hands all over my bare body.

Maybe I was already dead?

An electric shock started at the top of my head and moved all down through my body. It only took a second and at that precise moment I had a strange feeling that I would never have to take another drink again.

I picked up the phone and the motel woman's pleasant voice answered.

"What time is it, please?"

"It's two in the morning."

"I wonder if you would do me a favor?"

"Certainly," the woman replied.

"Would you please call Alcoholics Anonymous? I need help."

"I'd be very happy to."

In minutes the woman was at the door with a cup of tea. "I thought maybe you could use this until the people get here."

"You mean they're coming, for sure?"

"Yes. They're coming."

"Oh, thank God. I've given them so much trouble I didn't really think they'd bother. And thank you so much for the tea."

The short, plump, rosy-cheeked woman said, "Do you want me to stay with you until they get here?"

"Would you? I'm so sick."

I tried to hold the cup of tea and couldn't.

"Here, I'll help you hold it," the woman said.

It wasn't long before two AA women were at the door and the motel woman left.

"You've had it, huh?" one woman said.

"Yes, definitely. But I'm sure sick."

"Been through this before?"

"So many times I lost count."

"This can be the last time. You'll never have to be sick again."

"I can't go home. My husband will kill me."

"I'll take you to my house," the other woman said.

"Somebody took me in five years ago." The two women helped me into the car. It was slow going.

During the night I began vomiting and the woman brought a pail and set it beside the bed. The withdrawals had begun. The shaking, sweating, screaming, and pains in my stomach. Hot, cold, and my brain feeling as though it would pop.

My new friend patted me on the back. "You'll make it."

"I can't, Goddamn it. I can't."

"You're doing fine. I'm right here."

The second day was worse and my friend decided to call a doctor. He gave me a vitamin shot that helped some. When he left, my friend helped me into the bathroom again. There was a pressure, low in my belly, that made me have to urinate frequently. I knew it was the baby but my belly was still flat. My mind whirled about my past life, the children, and the unborn baby. I knew it was dead.

"Don't think about things like that now. Tomorrow you'll feel better," my friend told me.

"Will you call my husband and tell him I'm all right?"

Karl had turned me in to the police as a missing person. With great effort I called the police and told them I was all right and no longer missing.

"I'll have to go home tomorrow," I told my friend.

"Fine. I'll drive you and if you want me for anything be sure and call."

The next day I feebly got dressed and drank some orange juice and ate a few white crackers.

I thanked my friend for all her help and when I walked into my house there was no one there. Everything was in shambles and when the children wandered in one by one they didn't even speak.

I sat in the living room and faced reality for the first time in years. I had six children and I was pregnant and my life was a total wreck.

Karl came in and walked right to the kitchen. I followed and found dirty dishes piled high in and on the sink and on the table. I opened the refrigerator. Not much food, but a fifth of liquor. Karl pushed me away and grabbed the bottle. He poured himself a drink and waved the bottle under my nose.

142 "Don't you want a little drink?"

"No, I don't."

My mouth watered and became very dry.

"Come on, bitch, have a drink."

"Karl, the children."

"Ha! What the devil are you worried about the children for?"

"Give me a chance, Karl, please."

"Give you a chance? For thirteen years I've given you a chance. First off the bat I have to raise a bastard kid that belongs to someone else. And if that isn't enough, I go to Guam and you give me another one."

"Karl, Chris will hear you."

"I don't care. I gotta go out anyway."

"Karl, where're you going?"

"I got a date—how's that?"

"Please, Karl, don't leave me alone."

"Look, you'll be drunk in a few minutes, so why bother me?"

"I'd like to talk some things over with you."

"More of your problems? Do you know how many times I've listened to your problems? Do you know anything at all about what I've gone through all these years? Do you know how hard it's been for me? I've been in two wars, I've tried to make higher rates so we could have more money, and I've tried to make the Navy proud of me. I haven't done bad either, considering. The Navy is one place where I'm respected. All my men like me."

"All right, Karl, forget it."

"What's the use of trying to explain to you. You're either too drunk or sober and sanctimonious."

Karl left and I sat down again.

Maybe if I moved around it would help. A glass of water? I was so weak. I couldn't worry about Karl. My friend had said to do first things first.

I went to the kitchen and looked around. I made a decision to start. Doing something was better than doing nothing. I picked up a dirty spoon from the table and took it to the sink.

I did it! I moved the spoon to the sink!

I filled the sink with hot soapy water and with the sweat running out of every pore, I washed every dirty dish.

The spoon was the beginning. There were giant problems to solve but only one at a time. My children paid no attention to me and were running wild. I knew it would take time for them to believe in me and I didn't blame them. Karl was gone nearly a week and during that time I cleaned the house, washed the clothes, changed all the beds, and had things pretty well straightened. That was on the outside. It would take a long time to fix up the inside of me.

My women friends talked to me on the phone and dropped by to see me. Sometimes when things got too much, like bills, I'd sit down and try to do what my friends had told me.

"Turn it over to a Higher Power even if it's a doorknob."

I didn't know how—but it worked.

Minute by minute, hour by hour, I got better.

On the evening of the seventh day my children were all bathed and we were ready to watch tv. Karl came to the door, drunk.

"We're having a party. There's not enough room in the apartment we're in so we're moving over here. About twenty people and a couple of cases of beer."

I panicked.

Beer, people drinking, oh my God!

"Karl, please don't do this to me."

"Do what? Oh, you're on your pulpit again, I forgot. Well, it won't matter. If you're going to stay sober, you'll stay sober anyway, won't you?"

"Karl—"

"Look. I'm paying the rent here or did you forget? I'm telling you, I'm bringing the party here!"

I begged and pleaded but Karl would not change his mind. He went upstairs to the bathroom and then stormed out.

I didn't know what to do. Somewhere I had heard that if you need a prayer answered right away, it will be answered. I was desperate.

I ran upstairs to my bedroom, got down on my knees by the bed, and like a little child I prayed out loud.

"Dear God, whoever you are or whatever you are, I need a prayer answered right now. I heard that you can do this. Please, please help me, just this once. I need more time to get strong. Please don't let there be any drinking in this house. Amen."

144   Karl and his party didn't come back.

Gradually, as time passed, I forced myself not to think about the past and things got a little better. It didn't take long, with good food and rest, for my belly to pooch right out and I felt my baby kicking. That was a relief. At least it was alive.

My children were trying to help me. They harbored no resentments and when I had a bad day they encouraged me by saying, "You're doing fine, Mom."

They were listening to me and, for the first time in my role as mother, I listened to them.

January 20, 1959, Colleen was born. It was exciting for me because it was the first time I had ever watched one of my children being born. It was a natural childbirth and I felt, all through it, that I really wanted to sit up.

While I was in the hospital, Karl managed to stay home with the other children but as soon as I brought Colleen home, he started staying away again. It seemed like the longer I stayed sober the more he stayed away. I tried everything I knew to patch up the marriage and ended up feeling more and more trapped.

Finally I asked Karl for my identification and my driver's license, which he had been keeping for a long time.

"I'd like to get out of the house. Maybe go to the store."

He handed me my identification cards and my license. "Suppose you're planning on getting a bottle?"

"No, Karl. I'm not going to get a bottle. I just have to get out of this house."

I carefully slid into the front seat of the car and drove away. I was nervous and couldn't remember when I had driven a car cold sober. When I got to the shopping center I parked the car and walked briskly and confidently down the sidewalk. I was completely taken with the whole scene.

Look at all the people! All sizes and shapes and the colorful clothing! Wow, are they beautiful. And I can see the different colors of the cars. I never noticed before.

I went in the store and spoke to people I didn't even know, asking questions about where things were in the store, and everyone was willing to help. I picked up a fresh strawberry, put it to my nose, sucked in the delightful odor, and ate it. I put the groceries in the car and

145   took a walk around the shopping center. I looked in

the shop windows and once seeing my own image thought, "Not bad—considering."

I couldn't take my eyes off the people and marveled at reality. I hated to go home.

28

Karl was drinking more and more and I thought perhaps it was because he didn't have to worry about me any longer. I wanted to keep the family together and I attempted, several times, to talk to Karl.

"Can we have a talk, Karl?"

"What do you want to talk about?"

"Anything. Let's talk about the children."

"They're fine."

"Can we talk about us?"

"Get off my back with your nagging, will you?"

"Don't other men talk to their wives?"

"You've got friends to talk to. I don't know why women always want to carry on long conversations about things that don't matter a damn in this world!"

"They matter to me."

"Talk to your women friends then."

"Okay, Karl. I don't want to argue."

Deep down inside me I felt as though I were a half of a person. Like something was missing. The one thing that persisted was a feeling of being trapped with tons of responsibility. But somehow I felt it was really Karl who was preventing me from acting the way I wanted to. We disagreed on everything. He was strict disciplinarian and I was seeing that there were better ways to bring up children. I was doing a lot of reading and new ideas were creeping into my head. I realized, soon, that we were as different as two people could ever be.

Karl retired from the Navy in 1960 and we moved to what I believed to be our last home. Karl continued to drink and finally took a civilian job—traveling. He left the children and me alone again and when he did come home spent his nights out drinking with his buddies.

One Saturday morning he told all the children they were going on a boat ride with some friends of his.

I was in the kitchen and Mary and Tim came to me. They said they didn't want to go with Karl.

"Why not?"

"We just don't," Tim said.

Chris came in. "We really don't want to go, Mom. We've got other things to do."

"I don't understand."

"We're afraid of him," Mary admitted.

"Why?"

"He scares us when he's drinking, that's why," Tim said.

147

"You don't remember it but he used to take us for rides when you were drunk. Once he drove us up to the top of a mountain and right to the edge. We were really scared and Susan was crying," Chris said.

"Yeah?"

"Then he'd laugh and tell us we were sissies," Mary said.

"I'll see to it that you don't have to go," I said. "Run along and do what you want to do."

When Karl came into the kitchen, I was doing the dishes.

"Where's the kids? I'm ready to go. Hey, kids, come on, we're going," Karl yelled.

"They're not going, Karl."

"They're not going?"

"You heard me."

Karl puffed with anger. "What do you mean, they're not going? What the hell is this all about?"

"Just what I said; they don't want to go on a boat ride with you."

"What have you been telling them?"

"Nothing."

Karl raged. "Those kids are going with me! I told my buddy I'd bring them and they're going."

"They don't want to go, Karl."

"I told them to get ready and that was an order!"

"They're not in the Navy, Karl, and I told you they're *not* going."

"Why, you no-good drunken bitch! You and your god-damn reformed drunken friends!"

"Don't talk to me like that, Karl."

"You slut, I'll talk to you any way I want to."

I continued with the dishes, pulling my lips tight, and quietly said, "Karl, shut up."

In a second he raised his fist to hit me and before he had a chance I pulled a butcher knife from the dishwater and held it to his belly. He quickly stepped back.

"No, Karl. You're not going to hit me."

"Ha!"

"I mean it, Karl. Get back or I'll jam this knife right through your gut. In fact, you are *never* going to hit me again!"

Stunned, Karl fell back onto a kitchen chair.

I still held the knife in my hand.

"You never wanted to listen to me but you're going to listen now!"

"About what?"

I untied my apron and threw it on the floor.

"You can put the knife down. I'm not going to hit you," he said.

I dropped the long shiny butcher knife onto the floor and began tearing off my white blouse and brown skirt.

"What are you doing? My God, the children will see you!"

I stood naked. "So what? Weren't they all born from my womb? It's about time they saw me—the mother—all of me, for once! Of course they've always seen my mind—as screwed up as it was. And you—you saw nothing but my body—a piece of hamburger for you to fuck and for other men to rape—when they could catch me in a drunken stupor. You can all run free—while your babies pushed out from my body—crying for someone to love them."

I rubbed my hands all over my body. "Look, see, I have crawled out of the bottle—me—woman. Do you know how long I lived with guilt for all the things I've done? Trying all the time to play the role society said I should. Well, I'm through paying—and playing. I am going to be whole. I don't blame you because you're a victim too. But you liked your role and played it well. I want to think about something, though. Who punishes men for sending young boys to war to get killed? Who punishes men for destroying young minds and leaving thousands legless and armless—and yet they're against abortion? I'm an emotional woman, though, with not much to say and I'm not supposed to question or disapprove. I'm just a creature with no head. I bring boy babies into the world to grow up and get killed by their own fathers! 'Be a man—be patriotic!' But I have no head!"

I covered my head with my apron and I could see the children peeking and laughing.

"Come one, come all. Look at the creature with no head! But, ooohhhhh, what a body! Look at those breasts, those hips, those legs! If you will only honor them with one word—marriage—that body will fulfill her role and make a nest for you. A place for you to lay your head down after all the important works are done. The necessary works of war!"

"For God's sake, Nancy, shut up."

I couldn't stop. Every bit of anger I'd ever felt came rushing out.

"Then after you've rested and emptied yourself in that body, you can go back to your other home—your steel wombs bobbing around on Mother Nature's waters. The female ships, your safe and happy home-away-from-home. And all during the goddamn wars the women wait and wait and wait and the men convince them it's patriotic! Where's their medals? And the ones who don't wait are prostitutes—dirt—ostracized by society. No one questions what the men do."

"That's not my fault. I did the best I could."

"Oh yes, Karl. I know all about your uniformed lovers and how they verbally cut up women. And you listening. 'Poor Karl, married to that drunken woman.' "

"Who are you talking about?"

"The people you really cared for—your buddies!"

Karl was getting nervous. "Nancy, put your clothes on."

"No. I'm not going to put my clothes on, and take a good look, Karl. It's the last time you'll ever see me naked because the head belongs to the body and from now on I'm using my head. Alone and naked I came into this world, alone and naked I will die and what I do in between—from now on—is going to be up to me. Oh, God, is there a gentle, tender man?"

"And how do you plan to do all these things?"

"Obviously I'm going to divorce you. I'm through. I'm through being a slave to alcohol and through being a slave to you."

"Who in the hell is going to support you?"

"What? In the manner in which I'm accustomed to living under the military system?"

"After all the hell you put me through?"

"I've asked you before—why did you stay with me? Did you enjoy screwing me while I was unconscious?"

I was so relieved, I laughed and quoted:

There was a prospector named Dave,
Who kept a dead whore in a cave.

He said, "I'll admit, I'm a bit of a shit,
But look at the money I save."

Karl was furious. "You're absolutely, totally insane!"

"That's what they told my grandmother but they're not going to tell me that!"

The knife went limp and Karl got up. "You're serious?"

"Yes, Karl. I wish you all the happiness you can find and I mean it."

"I guess I'd better leave now?"

"I think it would be best."

"I'll pick up my clothes later. I've got a buddy I can stay—"

"I know, Karl."

After the front door closed I began putting my clothes back on. My torn blouse barely covered me and drips of perspiration fell off my nose. Chris opened the kitchen window and a gentle breeze blew in.

My children hugged and kissed my rumpled hair and my unmade-up face. Colleen put her head in my lap and I—I cried. I was no longer a prisoner. I was free.

About South End Press

South End Press is a nonprofit, collectively run book publisher with over 150 titles in print. Since our founding in 1977, we have tried to meet the needs of readers who are exploring or are already committed to the politics of radical social change. Our goal is to publish books that encourage critical thinking and constructive action on the key political, cultural, social, economic, and ecological issues shaping life in the United States and in the world. In this way, we hope to give expression to a wide diversity of democratic social movements and to provide an alternative to the products of corporate publishing.

If you would like to receive a free catalog of South End Press books or get information on our membership program—which offers two free books and a 40% discount on all orders for a year—please write to us at South End Press, 116 St. Botolph St., Boston, MA 02115.

Other Titles of Interest

A True Story of a Single Mother by Nancy Lee Hall

Race, Gender, and Work: a Multi-Cultural Economic History of Women in the United States by Teresa Amott and Julie Matthaei (Forthcoming in summer, 1990)

Poverty in the American Dream: Women and Children First by Karin Stallard, Barbara Ehrenreich, and Holly Sklar

Regulating the Lives of Women: Social Welfare Policy from Colonial Times to the Present by Mimi Abramovitz

Women and Male Violence: The Visions and Struggles of the Battered Women's Movement by Susan Schechter

Mink Coats Don't Trickle Down: The Economic Attack on Women and People of Color by Randy Albelda, Elaine McCrate, Edwin Melendez, and June Lapidus